EV 6,00

W9-BGF-527

The Liturgical Witness Of The New Testament

14 Worship Services Drawn From The New Testament

CHARLES M. MOUNTAIN

CSS Publishing Company, Inc.
Lima, Ohio

Library of Congress Cataloging-in-Publication Data

Mountain, Charles M., 1946-
    The liturgical witness of the Bible : 14 worship services drawn from the New Testament / Charles M. Mountain.
        p.   cm.
    Includes bibliographical references.
    ISBN 0-7880-0714-9 (pbk.)
    1. Worship programs. 2. Bible—Liturgical use. I. Title.
BV198.M68   1996
264—dc20   95-41228
                                                                          CIP

ISBN: 0-7880-0714-9   PRINTED IN U.S.A.

To Jane,

whose beauty, faithfulness,
hard work, and resilience
are surpassed by none

Table Of Contents

Introduction

This book is designed to provide "hands-on" worship services for use in conjunction with the Second Readings in the Revised Common Lectionary. The Church Year, as you know already, is built around the Gospel Reading. In the Season of Pentecost these readings are paired with the First Reading and are meant to give background or source material for the Gospel Reading. This is a good system and has fed the people of God for centuries.

The book you are now holding, however, breaks this pattern. It is not written as a criticism or rejection of the Gospel-led scripture readings. It is intended, rather, to help you, the preacher and/or worship planner, to employ more fully the weekly *Second* Reading as the basis for proclamation and liturgy. The use of continuous readings and preaching from the New Testament epistles has a long and honored history among many of the post-Reformation Christian traditions. This book attempts to return to these traditions as a parallel and complementary system of readings and preaching.

Moreover, this book is based on the liturgical material embedded in the Second Readings themselves. (The same principle holds for the services in this book derived from the Revelation of John, the Gospel According to Luke, and the Gospel According to John.) This book is an attempt to reemploy the very materials the writers of the Second Readings used and quoted, materials that had their origin in the then current worship practices of the early church.

Modern scholarship has made it clear that the New Testament is a unity expressed in a diversity. It is a unity in that its central focus is the incarnation, life, suffering, death, and the resurrection/ascension of Jesus Christ, with the subsequent sending of the Holy Spirit on the infant church. It is a diversity in that the New Testament was not written by one person. Nor did it issue from one congregation. The New Testament took shape over several decades by the hand of many authors in many places. Among the authors we can name are Paul and Peter, and James and John. The others, even the writers of the Gospels, are anonymous.

As a result there is a wide variety of forms used to express the central focus. The major forms of the New Testament are Gospel, pastoral letters, and apocalyptic. Within these larger forms we find smaller ones. The Gospels contain such forms as the parable, liturgical poetry, and discreet narratives (especially the Passion narrative). There are also a few hymns (for example, see John 1:1-18 or Luke's canticles). In the letters of Paul and others we find such things as hymns, credal statements, exhortations, proverbs called "topoi," "house rules," and so forth.[1] Revelation, not quite an apocalypse, has nonetheless many elements of the apocalyptic style: hymns, prophetic messages in the form of letters or in direct prophetic utterance, fantastic visions, theophanies, and the like.

II.

The Liturgical Witness Of The New Testament takes full advantage of these forms, large and small, to express unity by its use of the New Testament's diversity. The central focus is kept intact, but each New Testament book used is allowed to speak with its own voice. Take, for example, the service titled "Lordship And Unity: The Liturgical Witness Of Colossians" (pp. 89-100). The **Processional Hymn**, "Jesus Is The Image," is my versification of the Christ-hymn that Paul quotes in Colossians 1:14-20. The **Pastoral Greetings** is my translation of Colossians 1:2, a part of Paul's greeting. The **Dialogue**, originally part of a Baptismal liturgy, is used as an antiphonal proclamation of salvation, and the **Pastoral Assurance** (Colossians 1:21-22), originally Paul's interpretation of the hymn in Colossians 1:14-20, enforces its message. The **Confession of Faith** is my translation and formulation of various credal statements found in Colossians and Ephesians, namely, Colossians 1:12-15, 18-20 and Ephesians 1:20-23; 4:4. (The **Nicene Creed** is intended as an alternative confession.) The **Prayers** are my translation and adaptation of Paul's prayers in Colossians 3:12-15, ending with Colossians 3:4.

Interspersed among the Scripture Readings are short quotes of Colossians that seemed appropriate (3:16 and 3:17). The **Hymn of the Day** is another hymn that Paul quoted and I translated and versified, Colossians 2:13-14. The **Offertory Hymn** is a hymn Paul quotes in Ephesians 2:8-10. (Ephesians is Colossians' "twin sister," and their theological, Christological, and ecclesiastical concepts are very close.)

The **Words of Institution** and the **Lord's Prayer** are not quoted by Paul in Colossians. I have used the translation by the International Consultation on English Texts. The **Word of Exhortation** is a quote of Colossians 3:1-4, where Paul applies the Gospel to the situation of the Colossians — and ours!

The **Doxology** and the **Hymn** are not a part of Colossians. The **Doxology** is the well-known "Aaronic Blessing" (Numbers 6:24-26), and the **Hymn** is my versification of a portion of the prose work by Irenaeus, *Epideixis*, paragraph 34. I decided to use his words since they summarized the fundamental Christology of Colossians.[2] (The rest of the services based on the letters of the New Testament, of Revelation, and of the works of the Apostolic Fathers, including the *Didachê*, followed along the same lines.)

By now you may be asking with Luther, "What does this mean for us?" It means that when you come to Propers 10-13 in Series C of the Revised Common Lectionary, you have a "hands-on" liturgy made from the same letter from which you will be preaching. For four Sundays in a row, your congregation will be singing, praying, and gathering around the words and message of Colossians, and by means of Colossians drawing near to the One to which it bears witness. Your Sunday morning sermon will be brought home again and again. In addition, this service may be used on the last Sunday of the Church Year, Reign of Christ (Christ the King), and on any Sunday when the theme closely links our Lord's incarnation with his death and resurrection. The same may be said for most of the rest of the liturgies in this book, a few of which may be used several times a year.

III.

The first three services in this book, however, break the mold. The services based on Luke and John ("Through The Desert Clear A Highway!" and "The Bread Of Life," respectively), are my attempts to address what seems to me to be two cases of gross neglect in the Gospel-based Lectionary Readings. The service based on Luke is built around his canticles. (I call them Psalms.) These lyric poems express the centuries-long accumulation of the Jewish people's hopes for a Savior, a Christ. They are ideal for repeated use during the seasons of Advent and Christmas (that is, through January 6, The Epiphany of Our Lord). "The Bread Of Life" is my attempt to underline John's unique interpretation of the Holy Communion.

The third service, "Chorale Service Of Holy Communion," was made with the idea of bringing out the main themes of letters of Paul to the Romans and Galatians. After several unsuccessful attempts at versifying the various kinds of liturgical poetry they contain, I decided to use the hymns of Martin Luther and other Reformation hymn writers as the skeleton for a liturgy. The hymns chosen express, I believe, the essence of these particular Pauline letters very well. Moreover, this service will prove useful on such Festivals and Occasions such as Martin Luther, Renewer of the Church (February 18), Presentation of the Augsburg Confession, 1530 (June 25), Johann Sebastian Bach (June 28), Henry Melchior Muhlenberg, 1787 (October 7), Reformation Day (October 31), and not a few others.

One last note. Wherever possible, I have made my own translations, paraphrases, and versifications from the original languages of the Bible, especially the Greek New Testament and the Septuagint (LXX). I also made my own translations and paraphrases from the original German hymn texts of Martin Luther, Paul Speratus, and others. And the Greek texts of the Fathers were the basis for many of the hymns and other materials you will encounter.

Advent, 1995

---

1. These forms, by the way, are virtually the same in the Post-Apostolic Church [c. 90-150 CE]. They are found in the *Didachè* and in the letters of Ignatius and Clement, among others. See "In Death, True Life: The Liturgical Witness Of The Early Church," Chapter 14.

2. See also "A Living Hope: The Liturgical Witness Of First Peter," where I use the liturgical materials in 1 Peter and those of Melito of Sardis from his liturgical sermon, "On The Pasha."

1

The Liturgical Witness Of Luke
[Advent and Christmas Seasons, especially Series C]

"Through The Desert Clear A Highway!"

Service of Holy Communion

GATHERING

[Prelude]

STAND

Processional Hymn I

[First, Second, and Third Sundays in Advent]
"Comfort, Comfort Give My People"
Tune: *Freu Dich sehr,* 87 87 77 88
["Comfort, Comfort Ye My People"]

1.   Comfort, comfort give my people;
         softly to Jerus'lem speak.
     Tell her that the worst is over,
         that her God for her will seek.
     For her penalty is paid.
         God has full atonement made
     for each sin and all transgression;
         she is still God's sole possession.

11

2. Through the desert clear a highway,
   make the roadbed smooth and sound.
   Ev'ry valley must be filled in;
   grind the hills to level ground!
   For the glory of the Lord
   by this avenue's restored.
   God will do this, for God's spoken;
   and God's word cannot be broken!

3. On a high and massive mountain
   Zion heralds God's Good News.
   Shout out, hilltops of Jerus'lem:
   "God's Good News do not refuse!"
   Zion, raise your vibrant voice,
   and proclaim, "In God rejoice!"
   With this message are your feet shod:
   "Look and listen! This is your God!"

4. Look! Our conqu'ring king is coming;
   peace through all His Kingdom reigns.
   Rich rewards are coming with Him;
   He lost Paradise regains.
   Like a shepherd, He will feed
   all God's people in their need;
   little lambs the Lord will foster,
   and the nursing ewes will pasture.

Processional Hymn II

[Fourth Sunday in Advent, the Nativity of the Lord, and the Sundays after Christmas]

"My Soul Will Magnify The Lord"
Tune: *Veni, Emmanuel,* 88 88 88
["O Come, O Come, Emmanuel"]

1. My soul will magnify the Lord;
   in God my Savior I rejoice!
   For God Almighty did great things
   for me, God's lowly, "grace-full" choice.

O magnify God's holy name!
   God's mercy, Age to Age the same.

2. The Blessing One arose in strength,
   and scatter'd to the winds self-praise.
   Th'Almighty threw down thralldom's thrones
   that God the lowly high might raise!
   The hungry, poor, God will relieve;
   the rich will, empty, turn and leave.

3. God's servant, Israel, God has help'd,
   rememb'ring loyal, cov'nant love;
   our ancestors our God has bless'd,
   fulfilling faithful, loyal love.
   God speaks a steadfast, worthy word!
   Make great and magnify the Lord!

Dialogue

A: Arise and shine; your Light has come,
C: **and the Glory of the Lord has dawned upon you.**
For Darkness shall cover the earth,
   and thick Darkness the peoples;
but the Lord will rise upon you,
   and God's Glory you shall see.
The peoples shall come to your Dawning;
   and kings to your radiant Morning Light.

Confession of Faith

APOSTLES' CREED

**I believe in God, the Father almighty,
   creator of heaven and earth.**

**I believe in Jesus Christ, his only Son, our Lord.
   He was conceived by the power of the Holy Spirit
      and born of the virgin Mary.**

13

He suffered under Pontius Pilate,
  was crucified, died, and was buried.
He descended into hell.*
On the third day he rose again.
He ascended into heaven,
  and is seated at the right hand of the Father.
He will come again to judge the living and the dead.

I believe in the Holy Spirit, the holy catholic Church,
  the communion of saints,
  the forgiveness of sins,
  the resurrection of the body,
  and the life everlasting. Amen.

*Or, *He descended to the dead.*

Old Testament Canticle

"In God, The Lord, My Heart Exults"
Tune: *Chesterfield,* CM
["Hark The Glad Sound!"]

1. In God, the Lord, my heart exults;
     my God holds high my head;
   in God, my Savior, I rejoice:
     my foes came, saw — and fled!

2. No one is holy like the Lord,
     none like my Mountain strong!
   Besides the Lord there is no god —
     the Lord, my Rock and song!

3. Your boastful arrogance — let go;
     your prattling pride — be stayed!
   The Lord, our God, knows ev'rything;
     by God are actions weighed.

4. For in God's hands are life and death;
     the Lord makes poor or rich;
   God raises up, brings down to death —
     and low with high can switch!

14

5. God raises up the weak from dust,
    from refuse heaps, the poor;
    the barren one gets seven sons —
    the word of God is sure!

6. Our life and times are God's domain,
    who made earth's pillars strong.
    Upon them God has placed the world —
    and we to God belong!

Prayer of the Day

SIT

WORD

Scripture Readings

First Lesson

Psalm (Optional)

"O Praise The Living Lord, My Soul!"
Tune: *Consolation,* CM
["The King Shall Come When Morning Dawns"]

1. O praise the living Lord, my soul!
    O praise your God with song!
    With psalms I'll ever sing to God,
    with hymns, my whole life long!

2. O happy those whose help is found
    in Jacob's loving Lord,
    whose hope holds fast the hand of God,
    the God of Life restored.

3. God made the heav'ns and earth and sea,
    and all that in them moves.
    The Lord keeps faith forevermore;
    God's promise timeless proves!

15

4. The Lord God lifts those burdened down,
   and sets the captive free.
   The stranger finds a family;
   and those born blind can see.

5. God acts with justice, setting free
   from crushing servitude.
   God gives the hopeless heart release;
   God gives the hungry food.

6. The alien workers God protects,
   fights for their rights in court;
   provides the widow with her needs,
   to orphans gives support.

7. O Zion Mountain, your God reigns
   now and forevermore!
   In this Time and the Age to Come,
   praise God, the Lord adore!

Second Lesson

STAND

Before the Gospel Lesson, **all** say: **"Glory to God in the highest!"**

Gospel Lesson

After the Gospel Lesson, **all** say: **"To God's people, peace!"**

SIT

Sermon
[The sermon hymn may be sung before the sermon; another hymn may replace the hymn below:]

16

Hymn of the Day

"Give God The Glory!"
Tune: *Christe sanctorum,* 11 11 11 6
["Father, We Thank You"]

1. "Give God the glory!" — heaven high is hymning;
   "Peace to God's people!" — angels choir in concord.
   Bless'd be our great King, coming in the Lord's name!
      Hosanna! Sáve ús, Lord!

2. Bless we the Lord God, Israel's God, our Father,
   God has redeemed us from our sin and bondage.
   God raised up for us our kind King and Savior
      from David's linéáge.

3. Long time God promised, speaking through the
         prophets:
   "From foes God frees — from hate-full hands of
         tyrants!"
   Love constant, loyal, God has shown, rememb'ring
      God's holy Covénánts.

4. This is the oath God swore to father Abr'ham:
   "From foes your freedom!" — that we freely
         worship
   fearlessly, holy, righteously; thus living
      under God's leadership.

5. Making God's people ready for Christ's coming,
   John, Most High's prophet, goes before his Sov'reign,
   giving salvation's knowledge to God's people:
      forgiveness of their sin.

6. This is the tender mercy of the Highest:
   On those in Darkness, sitting in Death's shadow,
   blazes a Sunrise high above, bright shining;
      that they God's peace might know.

Offering
[An anthem, solo, or other music is appropriate here.]

STAND

Offertory

"Living God, Who Made The Heavens"
Tune: *Mendelssohn*, 77 77 D with refrain
["Hark, The Herald Angels Sing"]

> Living God, you made the heávéns,
>   this wide world, its salty seas.
> And as witness to your goódnéss,
>   you, for us, created these:
> Sprinkling rains, new seed to start;
>   harvest time, Spring's counterpart.
> Through these things you meet our needs;
>   with what joy you fill our heart!
>   *With your gifts we worship you,*
>   *faithful God, forever true!*

Offertory Prayer

ALL: O God of life, maker of all things, we thank you and acknowledge your goodness. You give us what is best through the products of the land and the work of human hands. Through them you meet our many needs. Accept the gifts we offer to you, taken from your world, and returned to you to be used for your glory, and for the benefit of those around us. Amen.

Prayers
[Other prayers, petitions and thanksgivings may be added to, or substituted for, the following]

A: Father, in this special season of the church year we give you thanks and praise for your best gift of all, Jesus Christ our Lord. For Christ is — as the angel Gabriel proclaimed — born of the Holy Spirit of the Most High, and was named the Son of God, our Savior from sin and death and the power of evil.
Lord, in your mercy,

18

C: hear our prayer.

A: Father, we read in the scriptures that "those who received the Word were baptized, and clung to the teaching, and to the gatherings, and to the breaking of bread." We too want to remain faithful to you, and to remain steadfast in a world that does not value you or your Word. Enable us to make worship, your teaching, the Sacrament, and the fellowship of your people the first priority in our lives. *Lord, in your mercy,*

C: hear our prayer.

A: Father, your Son, our Lord Jesus Christ, gave us this promise: "If you, even though full of sin, know enough to give good things to your children, how much more will the Father give the Holy Spirit to those who ask him." And so we ask: Give us your Holy Spirit, without whom we cannot believe in Jesus Christ or come to him — and without whom we cannot live in a way that honors Christ. *Lord, in your mercy.*

C: hear our prayer.

[After all petitions have been prayed, the Pastor then says:]

P: Father, into your hands we commit our lives and all our prayers.

C: Amen.

P: Let us pray together our Lord's prayer as it is found in Luke, chapter 11:

Father,
  hallowed be your name,
  your kingdom come,
  your will be done.
Give us today our daily bread.
Forgive us our sins,
  for we also forgive those indebted to us.
Save us from the time of trial.
  Amen.

Sharing of the Peace

SIT

MEAL

[If the Supper is not celebrated, the service continues with the Nunc dimittis (New Testament Canticle), below]

A: When the savior's hour had arrived,
   he sat down to eat with his disciples.
And he said to them,
"I have so much wanted
   to eat this Passover with you
      before my suffering!
Truly, I say to you,
   I will never eat it again
      until it is fulfilled in the Kingdom of God."

Taking the cup,
   Jesus gave thanks and said,
"Take this and share it among yourselves.
   I say to you that I will never drink
      of this fruit of the vine,
   until the Kingdom of God comes."

[Here the bread and wine are prepared in the full view of the congregation]

Words of Institution

P: And taking bread, he gave thanks,
      broke it, and gave it to them, saying,
         "This is my body which is given for you;
            do this for the remembrance of me."
   And likewise taking the cup after eating,
      he said,
   "This cup is the New Covenant in my blood,
      which is poured out for you."

20

SIT

Distribution

[Carols and hymns, and/or instrumental, choral, or solo music, may be used during the distribution]

STAND

Pastoral Blessing

P: "And he was made known to them
    in the breaking of bread" —
May the body and blood of our Lord Jesus Christ
    continue to strengthen your faith,
and enable you to serve God
    and those around you.

C: Amen.

New Testament Canticle

"O Lord, Your Servant Asks Release"
Tune: *Veni, Emmanuel,* 88 88 88
["O Come, O Come, Emmanuel"]

> O Lord, your servant asks release;
>   and, by your word, would go in peace.
> Salvation's face I've fully seen;
>   before our eyes you intervene!
> The Gentile's darkness will dispel;
>   and glory glows on Isráél.

SENDING

Benediction

P: The Lord bless you and protect you.
    The Lord's face shine on you
        and receive you with grace.

The Lord look upon you with favor,
and give you peace.

C: Amen.

<u>Hymn</u>

"The People Who In Darkness Walked"
Tune: *Vom Himmel hoch,* LM
["From Heaven Above To Earth I Come"]

1. The people who in Darkness walked
        have seen a great and glorious Light!
    On those who dwelt in Darkness deep,
        their "Son-Light" shines, dispelling Night!

2. In still increasing hope and joy
        your people, praising, lift their voice
    as in the time of harvest-joy,
        as those who split the spoil rejoice!

3. For God will break sin's slaving pow'r
        as in the days of Gideon,
    who with three hundred — far too few —
        destroyed the hosts of Midian!

4. For those with war-drummed warrior's tramp —
        who think to win with spears and swords —
    their blood-soaked clothes and boots will burn:
        The victory will be the Lord's!

5. For unto us a Child is born;
        to us God's only Son God grants,
    who'll rule with God's authority
        His names to us his glory chants:

6. Our *Wondrous Couns'lor, Mighty God,*
        whose *Everlasting Father's* love,
    will guide us as our *Prince of Peace,*
        to grant Shalom like that above.

7. His pow'r will grow in endless peace
   (the promise giv'n to David's throne),
   that he might show his righteousness.
   In this Child's face God's grace is known!

Sources for
"Through The Desert Clear A Highway!"
The Liturgical Witness Of Luke

Processional Hymn (Advent): Psalm 40:1-2, 9-11
Processional Hymn (4th Sunday in Advent, Christmas): Luke 1:46-55 *[Magnificat]*
Dialogue: Isaiah 60:1-3
Old Testament Canticle: 1 Samuel 2:1-8 *[Song of Hannah]*
Psalm: Psalm 146
Sermon Hymn: Luke 2:14; 19:38; 1:68-79 *[Gloria in excelsis + Benedictus]*
Offertory: Acts 14:15, 17
Offertory Prayer: Acts 14:15, 17
Lord's Prayer: Luke 11:2-4
Last Supper and Words of Institution: Luke 22:14-20
New Testament Canticle: Luke 2:29-32 *[Nunc dimittis]*
Benediction: Numbers 6:24-26
Hymn: Isaiah 9:2-7

Unless otherwise noted, all translations, paraphrases, and versifications are by Charles M. Mountain.

2

The Liturgical Witness Of John
[Propers 12-16, Series B; Holy Week]

"The Bread Of Life"

Service of Holy Communion

GATHERING

[Prelude]

STAND

<u>Entrance Hymn</u>

"Hymn To The Logos"
Tune: *Morecambe,* 10 10 10 10
["Spirit Of God, Descend Upon My Heart"]

1. In the beginning was the Word of God;
      the Word was with God, and the Word God was.
    From the beginning, He was there with God,
      Infinite Word, the first and primal Cause.

2. Through Him exist all things; apart from Him
      nothing was made, or infinite, finite;
    in Him was Life, or earthly, spiritual;
      He is the site of all new Life and Light.

3. Life and Light shine upon the Darker Realms;
   Darkness will neither grasp it, nor o'ercome;
   Light shines on earth, a world the Night o'erwhelms;
   Lit is the Light; the Darkness must succumb.

4. For this same Word both flesh and blood became —
   infinite God among us pitched a tent!
   We saw Christ's glory, glory as God's Son:
   God's grace and truth revealed in Christ's advent.

5. From His vast Fulness have we all received:
   infinite grace on grace from heaven sent.
   Moses received the Law; but grace and truth
   in Jesus Christ received embodiment.

Pastoral Greeting

P: Peace be with you.

C: And also with you.

P: Jesus said,
> *Peace I leave to you;*
> *my peace I give to you,*
> *not as the world gives, I give to you.*
> *Do not let your hearts be in turmoil,*
> *nor let them be fearful.*

C: Amen.

Dialogue

A: The hour has come
C: for the Son of Man to be glorified.
Amen, amen, I say to you, unless a grain of wheat
falls into the earth and dies,
it remains alone;
but if it dies,
it bears much fruit.
Those who love their life,
lose it;

and those who hate their life in this Age
  will preserve it for Eternal Life.
If any want to serve me,
  let them follow me —
and where I am,
  there my servant will be also.
Whoever serves me,
  the Father will honor.

Now is the Crisis of this Age;
  now the ruler of this Age will be thrown out.
And I, if I am lifted up from the earth,
  will draw all people to myself.

Prayer of the Day

SIT

WORD

Scripture Readings

Hebrew Bible Lesson: Exodus 16:1-8, 13-15

Psalm: Psalm 105:23-42

Communion Lesson: John 6:1-21 *[NRSV preferred]*

Sermon Text: *[This may be either the Lectionary reading or the Communion Lesson just read]*

Hymn of the Day
[or another appropriate hymn]

"Antiphon"
Tune: *Martyrdom,* CM
["Alas, And Did My Saviour Bleed?"]

1.　"My cherished Child, you're lifted up,
　　　'exalted' on a Tree!"
　　　　My Father, when I'm lifted up,
　　　　I'll draw all things to me.

27

2. "My cherished Child, you're 'glorified' —
    in shamed humility!"
    My shame, my Father, glorifies;
    my humbled pow'r sets free.

3. "My cherished Child, like Moses' snake
    you're fixed high on a pole!"
    My Father, only that they see
    my ensign, making whole.

4. "My cherished Child, to death poured out;
    like seed in soil you're sown!"
    My Father, though I die, I'll live —
    and I'll not rise alone!

5. "My cherished Child — a scapegoat sent,
    a blameless, slaughtered Lamb!"
    My Father, when I'm offered up,
    then all will know I AM.

6. "O chasten'd Christian, cherish'd child,
    look only to this Tree!"
    Here I my life for you gave free —
    the Tree's our victory!

Sermon

STAND

Confession of Faith

NICENE CREED

We believe in one God,
   the Father, the Almighty,
   maker of heaven and earth,
   of all that is, seen and unseen.

We believe in one Lord, Jesus Christ,
   the only Son of God,
   eternally begotten of the Father,

28

God from God, Light from light,
true God from true God,
begotten, not made,
of one Being with the Father.
Through him all things were made.
For us and for our salvation
he came down from heaven;
by the power of the Holy Spirit
he became incarnate from the virgin Mary, and was made
man.
For our sake he was crucified under Pontius Pilate;
he suffered death and was buried.
On the third day he rose again
in accordance with the Scriptures;
he ascended into heaven
and is seated at the right hand of the Father.
He will come again in glory to judge the living and the dead,
and his kingdom will have no end.

We believe in the Holy Spirit, the Lord, the giver of life,
who proceeds from the Father and the Son.
With the Father and the Son he is worshiped and glorified.
He has spoken through the prophets.
We believe in one holy catholic and apostolic Church.
We acknowledge one Baptism for the forgiveness of sins.
We look for the resurrection of the dead,
and the life of the world to come. Amen.

SIT

Offering
[An anthem, solo, or other music is appropriate here.]

STAND

Offertory Canticle

"John 3:16"
Tune: *Ellers,* 10 10 10 10
["Savior, Again To Thy Dear Name"]

1. As the bronze serpent Moses lifted up,
   so must the Son of Man be lifted up,
      that whosoever looks in faith on him
      may enter into God's eternal life.

2. This is the way God's love for us was shown:
   God gave the Son, the only one, God's own,
      that whosoever trusts and looks to him
      should never die, but have eternal life.

Prayers

Lord's Prayer

> **Our Father in heaven,**
> **hallowed be your name,**
> **your kingdom come,**
> **your will be done,**
> **on earth as in heaven.**
> **Give us today our daily bread.**
> **Forgive us our sins**
> **as we forgive those**
> **who sin against us.**
> **Save us from the time of trial**
> **and deliver us from evil.**
> **For the kingdom, the power,**
> **and the glory are yours**
> **now and forever. Amen.**

Sharing of the Peace

SIT

MEAL

[The ministers then prepare the bread and wine for distribution in full view of the congregation. After the bread and wine are ready, the Pastor and two assistants lead the congregation in the following liturgical arrangement of John 6:22-69]

Eucharistic Words from John

P: The next day the crowd that had stayed on the other side of the sea saw that there had been only one boat there. They also saw that Jesus had not gotten into the boat with his disciples, but that his disciples had gone away alone. Then some boats from Tiberias came near the place where they had eaten the bread after the Lord had given thanks. So when the crowd saw that neither Jesus nor his disciples were there, they themselves got into the boats and went to Capernaum looking for Jesus. When they found him on the other side of the sea, they said to him,

A1: "Rabbi, when did you come here?"

A2: Jesus answered them, "Very truly, I tell you, you are looking for me, not because you saw signs, but because you ate your fill of the loaves. Do not work for the food that perishes, but for the food that endures for eternal life, which the Son of Man will give you. For it is on him that God the Father has set his seal."

A1: Then they said to him, "What must we do to perform the works of God?"

A2: Jesus answered them, "This is the work of God, that you believe in him whom he has sent."

A1: So they said to him, "What sign are you going to give us then, so that we may see it and believe you? What work are you performing? Our ancestors ate the manna in the wilderness; as it is written, 'He gave them bread from heaven to eat.'"

A2: Then Jesus said to them, "Very truly, I tell you, it was not Moses who gave you the bread from heaven, but it is my Father who gives you the true bread from heaven. For the bread of God is that which comes down from heaven and gives life to the world.''

A1: They said to him, ''Sir, give us this bread always.''

A2: Jesus said to them,

[said]

P: ''I am the bread of life.
Whoever comes to me

C: will never be hungry,
and whoever believes in me
will never be thirsty.
But I said to you that you have seen me
and yet do not believe.
Everything that the Father gives me will come to me,
and anyone who comes to me I will never drive away;
for I have come down from heaven, not to do my own will,
but the will of him who sent me.

[sung by all] (Tune: *St. Clement,* 98 98)

1. ''This is the will of God who sent me:
that all whom God will send my way,
not one of them will die — no, never —
and I will raise them ón thé Lást Day.

2. ''This is my Father's will and longing:
that all may God's own Son survey,
and have in this life Life Eternal —
and I will raise them ón thé Lást Day.''

A1: Then the Jews began to complain about him because he said, ''I am the bread that came down from heaven.'' They were saying, ''Is not this Jesus, the son of Joseph, whose father and mother we know? How can he now say, 'I have come down from heaven'?''

A2: Jesus answered them, ''Do not complain among yourselves.

[sung by all]

3. "To come to me no man is able;
    to come to me, no woman may,
    unless the One who sent me draws them —
    and I will raise them ón thé Lást Day.

A2: "It is written in the prophets, 'And they shall all be taught by God.' Everyone who has heard and learned from the Father comes to me. Not that anyone has seen the Father except the one who is from God; he has seen the Father.

[said]

P: Very truly, I tell you, whoever believes has eternal life.
C: **I am the bread of life.**
Your ancestors ate the manna in the wilderness,
    and they died.
This the bread that comes down from heaven,
    so that one may eat of it and not die.
I am the living bread that came down from heaven.
    Whoever eats of this bread will live forever;
    and the bread that I will give for the life of the world
    is my flesh."

A1: The Jews then disputed among themselves, saying, "How can this man give us his flesh to eat?"
A2: So Jesus said to them, "Very truly, I tell you, unless you eat the flesh of the Son of Man and drink his blood, you have no life in you.

[sung by all]

4. "All those who take and eat my body,
    all those who will my blood assay,
    have now, in this life, life eternal —
    and I will raise them ón thé Lást Day."

[said]

P: "For my flesh is true food
C: **and my blood is true drink.**
Those who eat my flesh and drink my blood
abide in me, and I in them.
Just as the living Father sent me,
and I live because of the Father,
so whoever eats me
will live because of me.
This is the bread that came down from heaven,
not like that which your ancestors ate,
and they died.
But the one who eats this bread will live forever."

A1: He said these things while he was teaching in the synagogue at Capernaum. When many of his disciples heard it, they said, "This teaching is difficult; who can accept it?"

A2: But Jesus, being aware that his disciples were complaining about it, said to them, "Does this offend you? Then what if you were to see the Son of Man ascending to where he was before?

[said]

P: "It is the spirit that gives life;
C: **the flesh is useless.**
The words that I have spoken to you
are spirit and life.

A2: But among you there are some who do not believe."
A1: For Jesus knew from the first who were the ones that did not believe, and who was the one that would betray him.
A2: And he said, "For this reason I have told you that no one can come to me unless it is granted by the Father."
A1: Because of this, many of his disciples turned back and no longer went about with him.
A2: So Jesus asked the twelve, "Do you also wish to go away?" Simon Peter answered him,

[sung by all]

5. "O Lord, who else need we be seeking?
   Eternal life is in your word!
   We have believed — and still acknowledge —
   you are God's Holy One, our Lord!"

STAND

Words of Institution

P: In the night in which he was betrayed,
our Lord Jesus took bread and gave thanks;
broke it, and gave it to his disciples, saying,
"Take and eat; this is my body, given for you.

Do this for the remembrance of me."

Again, after supper,
he took the cup, gave thanks
and gave it for all to drink, saying,
"This cup is the new covenant in my blood,
shed for you and for all people
for the forgiveness of sins.

Do this for the remembrance of me."

SIT

Distribution

*[Congregational hymns, instrumental or vocal music may be used during the distribution. As the bread and wine are distributed, **one or more** of the following passages may be read by one of the assistants: John 13:31-35; or John 14:1-3, 6-7; or John 14:15-21, 23; or John 15:1-11; or John 15:12-17; or John 16:7-11; or John 16:20-24; or John 17:1-5; or John 17:6-19; or John 17:20-26. Hymns may be sung as well]*

STAND

Pastoral Blessing

P: May the Bread of Life,
  and the New Wine of the Spirit,
strengthen your faith,
  and enable you to abide in Christ,
    who abides in you by faith.

C: Amen.

SENDING

A1: When Jesus presented himself alive
  to the disciples after his resurrection,
he said, "Peace be with you!"
  Then he showed them his hands and side.

A2: Then he said,
  "Peace be with you!
    As the Father sent me,
      just so I send you."

A1: As we go, let us with Thomas
  also confess Jesus as:

C: "My Lord and my God!"

Canticle

"From Death To Life"
Tune: *Brother James' Air,* 86 86 86
["The Lord's My Shepherd"]

1.　"Amen, amen, I say to you,
    the one who hears my word,
  and who believes in God who sent me,
    has Eternal Life;
  and is not judged, but has pass'd o'er
    from Death to Eternal Life.

36

2. "I am the Resurrection, and
        I am the Source of Life.
    Those who believe in me, e'en though
        they die, yet shall they live;
    and all who live and trust in me
        shall never, ever die."

Sources for
"The Bread Of Life"
The Liturgical Witness Of John

Entrance Hymn: John 1:1-5, 9, 14, 16-17
Pastoral Greeting: John 20:19; 16:27
Dialogue: John 12:23-28, 30-33
Hymn of the Day: Isaiah 52:13—53:12
Offertory Canticle: John 3:16-17
Lord's Prayer: International Consultation on English Texts.
Eucharistic Words of John: John 6:22-70 (NRSV, except for the five ver-
    sifications)
Dismissal: John 20:19-23, 28
Canticle: John 5:24; 11:25-26

Unless otherwise acknowledged, all translations, paraphrases, and versifi-
    cations from the Greek New Testament are by Charles M. Mountain.

3

The Liturgical Witness Of Romans And Galatians

and for
Martin Luther, Renewer of the Church (February 18),
Presentation of the Augsburg Confession, 1530 (June 25),
Johann Sebastian Bach (June 28),
Henry Melchior Muhlenberg, 1787 (October 7),
and others.

*[Lent, Series A; Propers 7-19, Series B; Propers 4-9;
Series C; Reformation Day]*

Chorale Service
Of Holy Communion

(following the order of *The German Mass* by Martin Luther)

STAND

Entrance Hymn

"A Mighty Fortress Is Our God"
Tune: *Ein' feste Burg,* 87 87 66 667

1.   A mighty fortress is our God,
     a solid bulwark and defense;
     God moves to help us in our need
     so imminent and so immense!
        For our malicious Foe
        still seeks to work us woe;
        great powér and deceit
        he wields for our defeat.
     On earth is not the like of him!

2. Our war with him had scarce begun
   when we were lost and left undone!
   But fights for us a Champion
   who God chose — who the war has won.
   You ask then, "Who is he
   who fought to set us free?"
   Lord Jesus Christ, his name;
   through him, your life reclaim!
   As true God, Christ the field has seized!

3. Though ev'ry evil in this world
   should threaten to devour us,
   we need not ever yield to fear:
   no pow'r have they to o'erpow'r us.
   The Prince of this Old Age,
   though bitterly he rage,
   can nothing to us do.
   This means that he is through.
   A little Word can fell him.

4. The Word then will forever stand —
   no thanks to ancient enemies.
   God gave the Spirit and the gifts,
   and in the end the field will seize.
   If they then seize our life —
   house, honor, child or wife —
   well, let them take them all!
   They've nothing gained at all.
   God's Kingdom with us still remains.

Apostolic Greeting

P: Grace and peace to you,
from God our Father,
and our Lord, Jesus Christ.

C: Amen.

P: Let us confess our sins by singing the following hymn:

Kyrie

"From Deepest Need"

Tune: *Melita,* 88 88 88
["Eternal Father, Strong To Save"]

1. From deepest need I cry to you,
   O Lord God, hear and heed my cry!
   O turn a gracious ear to me,
   my urgent prayer do not deny.
   > If you regard our sin and wrong,
   > who could you rightly justify?

2. With you will only grace prevail
   that you our sense of sin erase!
   With you good works will not avail —
   sin will the best of lives deface!
   > The bold and foolish, let them boast;
   > but you we fear — and love your grace.

3. And so I hope in God alone,
   and not on my own virtues build.
   On God my heart will heedless lean —
   the God who's good, whose Word good willed.
   > This is my comfort and my shield;
   > my anxious heart by hope is stilled.

4. Though watching wakeful through the night,
   then watching weary through the day,
   my heart will still in God's will trust;
   no doubt or worry will me sway.
   > Thus does true Israel, Spirit-born,
   > who hopes in God, let come what may.

5. It's true that we are full of sin;
   yet God with grace is flowing o'er!
   God's helping hand no hindrance knows,
   though shame wells up within our core.
   > Good Shepherd, gracious God, forgive
   > your Israel's sins, her life restore!

41

Absolution

P: For the sake of the life, death, and resurrection of Jesus Christ,
I declare to you the entire forgiveness of all your sins.

C: Thanks be to God!

Hymn of Praise

"Christ Jesus Lay Dead, Bound By Death"
[Stanzas 1-4]
Tune: *Christ lag in Todesbanden,* 87 87 78 74

1. Christ Jesus lay dead, bound by Death,
for our sins given over.
But we with Christ were raised to Life;
Life's war is striven, over!
Therefore let us thankful be,
give praise to God, and joyfully
together sing, "Alleluia!"
Alleluia!

2. No one has ever conquered Death,
no mortal man or woman.
For Sin, the root cause of our state,
caused weakness all too human.
Therefore Death came rushing in,
and held us captive in his reign.
So soon Death seized dominion!
Alleluia!

3. Christ Jesus, God's belovéd Son,
was born of mortal woman,
from Sin has freed, has Death undone,
restored our state as human!
Death no longer o'er us lords;
he threatens us with empty words.
Death's sting is lost forever!
Alleluia!

4. And when these Champions met to fight
   a fearful combat followed;
   but in the end, Life held the field,
   for Death by Life was swallowed!
       Scriptures long since loud proclaim:
       the one death swallows Death and shame.
   Death now is nothing but a hoax!
       Alleluia!

or

"Dear Christians, One And All, Rejoice"
[Stanzas 1-4]
Tune: *Nun freut Euch,* 87 87 887

1. Dear Christians, one and all, rejoice,
       With exultation springing.
   And, with united heart and voice
       And holy rapture singing,
   Proclaim the wonders God has done,
   How God's right hand the vict'ry won!
       What costly price our ransom!

2. Fast bound in Satan's chains I lay,
       Death brooded darkly o'er me,
   Sin was my torment night and day;
       in sin my mother bore me.
   But daily deeper still I fell;
   My life was then a living hell,
       So firmly sin possessed me.

3. My own good works all came to naught,
       No grace or merit gaining;
   Free will against God's judgment fought,
       Dead to all good remaining.
   My fears increased till sheer despair
   Left only death to be my share;
       The pangs of hell I suffered.

43

4. But God had seen my wretched state
   Before the world's foundation,
   And, mindful of more mercies great,
   God planned for my salvation.
   God turned to me a father's heart;
   God did not choose the easy part,
   But gave God's dearest treasure.

or

"Dear Christians, One And All, Rejoice"
[Stanzas 5-8]
Tune *Nun freut Euch*, 87 87 887

5. God said to the belovéd Son:
   " 'Tis time to have compassion.
   Then go, bright jewel of my crown,
   And bring to all salvation;
   From sin and sorrow set them free;
   Slay bitter death for them that they
   May live with you forever."

6. The Son obeyed his Father's will,
   Was born of virgin mother;
   And, God's good pleasure to fulfill,
   He came to be my brother.
   His royal pow'r disguised he bore,
   A servant's form, like mine, he wore,
   To lead the devil captive.

7. To me Christ said, "Stay close to me,
   I am your rock and castle.
   Your ransom I myself will be;
   For you I strive and wrestle;
   For I am yours, and you are mine,
   For where I am you may remain;
   the foe shall not divide us.

8. "Though sin will shed my precious blood,
   Of life me thus bereaving,
All this I suffer for your good;
   Be steadfast and believing.
Life will from death the vict'ry win;
My innocence shall bear your sin;
   And you are blest forever."

Salutation

P: The Lord be with you.

C: **And also with you.**

P: Let us pray.

Prayer of the Day

SIT

Scripture Readings

First Lesson

Psalm

Second Lesson

STAND

Gospel Lesson

SIT

Sermon Hymn

[This or another hymn may be sung after the sermon]

"Law And Gospel"
Tune: *Es ist das Heil,* 87 87 887
["Salvation Unto Us Has Come"]

1. Salvation unto us has come
       through God-giv'n grace and goodness.
   Law will not to our works succumb;
       there is no end to "should-ness."
   Our faith is fixed on Christ alone
   whose work is our chief cornerstone.
       Christ is our Mediator.

2. What we must do, God's Law commands,
       but gives no pow'r to do it.
   Then wrath wells up and reprimands,
       for Law demands what's due it.
   Though we at times Law's form can keep,
   to Law's true spirit we're asleep.
       Forlorn and lost, we flounder.

3. For we, in sin's dream-revery,
       confuse the Law for Gospel —
   as if we can ourselves make free
       by willing life eternal!
   The Law, a mirror, makes it plain
   what evils in our heart remain.
       Great sin hides in our nature.

4. Still, all the law must be fulfilled.
       (Yet how can we, corrupted?)
   So God, in love, to save us willed;
       Life in our death erupted!
   For, in the Person of the Son,
   the Father Life for us has won.
       The Wrath dooms us no longer.

46

5. No more let doubt disturb your peace;
    God's Word will not betray you.
From death's despair receive release;
    let nothing more dismay you:
"All who believe and are Baptized
will see salvation realized."
    To life have they passed over.

Sermon

STAND

Prayers

Sharing of the Peace

SIT

Offering
[An anthem, solo, or other music is appropriate here]

STAND

Offertory

"Now Thank We All Our God"
Tune: *Nun danket alle Gott,* 67 67 66 66

1. Now thank we all our God,
    With heart and hands and voices,
Who wondrous things hath done,
    In whom this world rejoices;
Who from our mother's arms
    Hath blessed us on our way
With countless gifts of love,
    And still is ours today.

2. Oh may this bounteous God
        Through all our life be near us,
    With ever joyful hearts
        And blesséd peace to cheer us;
    And keep us in God's grace,
        And guide us when perplex'd,
    And free us from all ills
        In this world and the next.

3. All praise and thanks to God
        The Father, now be given,
    The Son, and Spirit sent,
        With them in highest heaven,
    The One eternal God,
        Whom earth and heav'n adore,
    For thus it was, is now,
        And shall be evermore!

Great Thanksgiving

P: The Lord be with you.
C: **And also with you.**
        Lift up your hearts.
        We lift them up to the Lord.
        Let us give thanks to God.
        This is only right to do.

Preface

[all sing]

"Here Is The True Passover Lamb"
[Stanzas 5-7]
Tune: *Christ lag in Todesbanden,* 87 87 78 74

5. Christ is the true Passover Lamb
    of which God's Word has boasted,
    who has, high up upon the Tree,
    in burning love been roasted!
        Christ's blood clearly marks the door,
        and Death's repelled forevermore.

The butcher cannot reach us!
Alleluia!

6. This High Feast let us celebrate
with joy — for this God pleases.
The Lord himself will shine on us;
for as the sun, so he is.
    Dazz'ling Christ, by force of grace,
      the Darkness to your Light gives place.
The Night of Sin has passed-o'er us!
Alleluia!

7. Then let us eat the Living Bread,
the Bread come down from heaven.
God's Word must purge the dead yeast out,
that old, malicious leaven.
    Only Christ will be the food
      that really feeds our souls with good.
By Christ faith lives, by Christ alone!
Alleluia!

P: Help us now, heavenly Father, to join with the hosts of heaven,
as they worship you without ceasing, day and night:

Sanctus

"I Saw The Lord"
Tune: *Forest Green,* CMD
["I Sing The Mighty Power Of God"]

1. I saw the Lord, high, lifted up,
and seated on a throne;
and, all around, God's entourage
called out the other's tone:
    "Sing, 'holy, holy, holy, Lord,
      the God of heaven's hosts;
    this whole wide world, from coast to coast,
      of God's great glory boasts.' "

2. The Seraphs formed this heav'nly choir;
   with wings of thunder-stroke;
   and when they sang, the Temple shook;
   the House was filled with smoke!
   > "O woe is me! I'm surely lost!
   > I sin in speech the most!
   > Yet with my eyes I've seen the King,
   > the Lord of heaven's host!"

3. But then a Seraph flew to me,
   a live coal in its hand,
   and touched my lips with heaven's fire
   that 'fore God I might stand.
   > "God's holy fire has purged your lips;
   > your guilt has gone away.
   > Your sin too has been blotted out —
   > now God alone obey!"

Words of Institution

P: In the night in which he was betrayed,
our Lord Jesus took bread and gave thanks;
broke it, and gave it to his disciples, saying,
"Take and eat; this is my body, given for you.

Do this in remembrance of me."

Again, after supper,
he took the cup, gave thanks
and gave it for all to drink, saying,
"This cup is the new covenant in my blood,
shed for you and for all people
for the forgiveness of sins.

Do this for the remembrance of me."

Lord's Prayer

Agnus Dei

"O Lamb Of God Most Holy!"
Tune: *O Lamm Gottes,* 77 77 777

1., 2. O Lamb of God most holy!
Who on the Cross once suffered,
And patient still and lowly,
Yourself to scorn once offered;
Our sins by you were taken,
Or hope had us forsaken:
have mercy on us, Jesus! *(Repeat)*

3.   O Lamb of God most holy!
Who on the Cross once suffered,
And patient still and lowly,
Yourself to scorn once offered;
Our sins by you were taken,
Or hope had us forsaken:
Your peace be with us, Jesus! Amen.

SIT

Communion

STAND

Pastoral Blessing

P: The Body and Blood of our Lord Jesus Christ strengthen and keep you safe unto eternal life.

C: Amen.

Post-Communion Hymn

"God Be Praised"
Tune: *Gott sei Dank,* 77 77
["Spread, O Spread, Thou Mighty Word"]

1.   God be praised, and God be thanked;
God feeds us with heav'nly food!
God in Christ — our flesh and blood:
Give us these, Lord, for our good.

2. Jesus, made our flesh and blood,
   formed by God — this is our creed —
   in maid Mary's human womb:
   Help us in our human need!

3. Greater love can no one show
   when to death, that we might live,
   was your holy body giv'n:
   Christ, our heartfelt thanks we give!

4. Grant us, Lord, your blessing pure
   that in oneness, trust, and love
   we may follow all your ways:
   Send us manna from above.

5. May your Spirit ne'er us leave!
   Grant to us Christ's heart and mind,
   that your Christendom belov'd
   peace and love and oneness find.

Benediction

P: The Lord bless you,
     and keep you.
   The Lord's face shine upon you,
     and be gracious to you.
   The Lord's countenance be lifted upon you,
     and give you peace.

C: **Amen.**

Hymn

"May God Gracious Be To Us"
Tune: *St. George's Windsor,* 77 77 D
["Come, You Thankful People, Come"]

1. May God gracious be to us,
     and upon us shine with grace.
   May God's ways be known on earth;
     may all peoples see God's face!

For when God's great works are shown,
   then what pleases God is known.
Christ, salvation manifest,
   turn us back to God most blest!

2. Let the peoples give you thanks,
      and sing out with all their voice!
   Let them sing their praise, O God!
      Let the world in you rejoice!
   You are Judge, and Sin restrain;
      Sin will never have free rein!
   Your strong Word is shield and guide —
      e'en for those who from you hide!

3. All the peoples thank you, Lord,
      for the land brings forth and grows.
   They will praise you with good works.
      (From your Word best counsel flows.)
   Give our spirits Life again
      as we cry aloud, "Amen!"
   Bless us, Father; bless us, Son;
      bless us, Spirit, three in One.

Sources for
Chorale Service Of Holy Communion
The Liturgical Witness Of Romans And Galatians
[for use with the Scripture Readings
from Romans and Galatians]

Entrance Hymn: *Ein' feste Burg ist unser Gott,* Martin Luther (tr. CM)
Kyrie: *Aus tiefer Not schrei ich zu Dir,* Martin Luther (tr. CM)
Hymn of Praise: *Christ lag in Todesbanden,* Martin Luther (tr. CM);
  or *Nun freut euch,* Martin Luther (tr. Richard Massie)
Sermon Hymn: *Es ist das Heil uns kommen her,* Paul Speratus (tr. CM)
Offertory: *Nun danket alle Gott,* Martin Rinkart (tr. Catherine Winkworth)
Sanctus: Isaiah 6:1-7 (paraphrase, CM)
Words of Institution: International Consultation on English Texts
Angus Dei: *O Lamm Gottes,* Nikolaus Decius (tr. Arthur Tozer Russell)
Post-Communion Hymn: *Gott sei gelobed und gebendeiet,* Martin Luther
  (tr. CM)
Hymn: *Es woll uns Gott gnädig sein,* Martin Luther (tr. CM)

Unless otherwise noted, all translations, paraphrases, and versifications are
by Charles M. Mountain.

4

The Liturgical Witness Of
The Corinthian Letters

*[Epiphany 4-8, A; Epiphany 2-9, B; Epiphany 2-8, C;
Transfiguration, BC; Ash Wednesday, ABC;
Holy Thursday, ABC;
Resurrection of the Lord; Propers 4-9, B]*

"One Lord, One Body"

Service of Holy Communion

GATHERING

[Prelude]

STAND

Entrance Hymn

"The Love Of Christ Constrains Us"
Tune: *Aurelia,* 76 76 D
["The Church's One Foundation"]

1. The love of Christ constrains us
  to publish far and wide
 that, since all people perished,
  then Christ for all has died.
 And joined to Christ, we living,
  who once in sins were dead,

live for ourselves no longer,
 but live in Christ, our Head.

2. From now on we view no one
  from human points of view,
 for people in Christ Jesus
  are creatures wholly new!
 For God's New Re-Creation
  our God with Life endures;
 the Old Creation perished,
  and God the New renews!

3. Our God was reconciling,
  through Christ, this wayward world,
 not counting accusations
  the Law against them hurled.
 For our sake God made Jesus,
  though sinless, sin to be,
 that we might then be righteous,
  and from Law's judgment, free.

Pastoral Greeting

P: Grace to you and peace
  from God the Father
   and the Lord Jesus Christ.

C: **Amen.**

Dialogue

A: If I speak in the tongues of mortals and of angels, but
  do not have love,
C: **I am a noisy gong or a clanging cymbal.**
 And if I have prophetic powers,
  and understand all mysteries and all knowledge,
 and if I have all faith, so as to remove mountains,
  but do not have love,
 I am nothing.

If I give away all my possessions,
   and I hand over my body so that I may boast,
but do not have love,
   I gain nothing.

Love is patient;
   love is kind;
love is not envious or boastful
   or arrogant or rude.
It does not insist on its own way;
   it is not irritable or resentful;
It does not rejoice in wrongdoing,
   but rejoices in the truth.
It bears all things,
   believes all things,
hopes all things,
   endures all things.
ALL: **Love never ends.**

But as for prophecies,
   they will come to an end;
as for tongues,
   they will cease;
as for knowledge,
   it will come to an end.
For we know only in part,
   and we prophesy only in part;
but when the complete comes,
   the partial will come to an end.
When I was a child,
   I spoke like a child,
I thought like a child,
   I reasoned like a child;
when I became an adult,
   I put an end to childish ways.
For now we see in a mirror, dimly,
   but then we will see face to face.

Now I know only in part;
then I will know fully,
even as I have been fully known.

And now faith, hope, and love abide, these three;
and the greatest of these is love.

Prayer of the Day

SIT

WORD

Scripture Readings

[Music is appropriate before or after any of the readings]

First Lesson

[Read before the Psalm]

When you come together,
each one has a hymn,
a lesson, a revelation,
a tongue or an interpretation.
Let all things be done for building up;
for God is not a God of chaos,
but of peace.

Psalm *[Preferably sung; Psalm 105:1-6, 37-45 is suggested]*

[Read before the Second Lesson]

Just as the body is one
and has many members,
and all the members of the body,
though many,

are still one body —
    so is Christ.
For by the one Spirit
    we were all Baptized
        into one Body.

Second Lesson

STAND

[Read before the Gospel Lesson]

The word of the Cross
    is meaningless to those
        who are perishing;
but to us who are being saved
    it is the power of God.

Gospel Lesson

SIT

<u>Hymn of the Day</u>

Sermon

STAND

<u>Confession of Faith</u>

A: [Saint Paul wrote these words:]
    Now I make known to you, brothers and sisters,
        the Gospel that I proclaimed to you,
    which also you received,
        in which also you stand,
    through which also you are saved —
        if you hold fast to the word that I proclaimed to you;
    for I handed down to you as of first importance
        which also I received.

C: **Christ died for our sins**
in accordance with the scriptures,
and was buried;
and he was raised on the third day
in accordance with the scriptures,
and he appeared to Peter,
then to the twelve.

or

[Sung] **"One God, One Lord"**
Tune: *Laude Domini,* 666 666
["When Morning Gilds The Skies"]

There is one God, the Father,
from whom were all things made,
and for whom we exist;
and one Lord, Jesus Christ,
through whom were all things made,
through whom we all exist.

or

NICENE CREED

We believe in one God,
the Father, the Almighty,
maker of heaven and earth,
of all that is, seen and unseen.

We believe in one Lord, Jesus Christ,
the only Son of God,
eternally begotten of the Father,
God from God, Light from light,
true God from true God,
begotten, not made,
of one Being with the Father.
Through him all things were made.

60

For us and for our salvation
he came down from heaven;
by the power of the Holy Spirit
he became incarnate from the virgin Mary, and was made
man.
For our sake he was crucified under Pontius Pilate;
he suffered death and was buried.
On the third day he rose again
in accordance with the Scriptures;
he ascended into heaven
and is seated at the right hand of the Father.
He will come again in glory to judge the living and the dead,
and his kingdom will have no end.

We believe in the Holy Spirit, the Lord, the giver of life,
who proceeds from the Father and the Son.
With the Father and the Son he is worshiped and glorified.
He has spoken through the prophets.
We believe in one holy catholic and apostolic Church.
We acknowledge one Baptism for the forgiveness of sins.
We look for the resurrection of the dead,
and the life of the world to come. Amen.

SIT

Offering

[An anthem, solo, or other music is appropriate here]

STAND

Offertory Canticle

"How Great The Grace Of Christ!"
Tune: Heath, SM
["We Give Thee But Thine Own"]

How great the grace of Christ!
Though rich, himself made poor,
that — for our sakes — his poverty
might make us very rich!

61

Offertory Prayer

C: **God our father, accept these gifts we offer, only a small part of all that you have given us. May they meet the needs — physical, emotional, mental, spiritual — of those who use them. May they, as precious seeds, reap a harvest of praise and thanks to you, from whom all blessings flow. Amen.**

Prayers and the Sharing of the Peace

[The ministers then prepare the bread and wine for distribution]

MEAL

Great Thanksgiving

P: The Lord be with you.
C: **And also with you.**
Lift up your hearts.
We lift them up to the Lord.
Let us give thanks to the Lord our God.
It is right to give him thanks and praise.

Preface

P: It is right that we praise and thank you, heavenly Father, for your love and mercy, especially the mercy shown to us in the sending of your Son, Jesus Christ, our Lord:

For the same God who said,
"Out of Darkness, let there be Light,"
is the one who has shined in our hearts,
giving us the knowledge of God's glory
in the face of Jesus Christ.

Enlighten our hearts, O Father,
  through the power of the Holy Spirit,
and enable us to join with the hosts of heaven,
   and your whole church on earth,
as they unite in the song
  which never ceases, day or night:
    [To the "Holy, Holy, Holy," *below]*

or

P: It is right that we praise and thank you, heavenly Father,
for your love and mercy, especially the mercy shown to
us in the sending of your Son, Jesus Christ, our Lord:

For in Christ's death and resurrection,
  and in this holy supper,
we see the fulfillment of the New Exodus
  on our behalf:

   For our ancestors were all under the cloud,
     and all passed through the sea,
   and all were baptized into Moses
     in the cloud and the sea;
   and all ate the same spiritual food,
     and all drank the same spiritual drink.
   For they drank from the spiritual rock
     that followed them —
       and that rock was Christ.

Give us now your Holy Spirit,
  and enable us to join with the hosts of heaven,
and your whole church on earth,
  as they unite in the song
    which never ceases, day or night:

Sanctus

"Holy, Holy, Holy"
Tune: *Nicaea,* 11 12 12 10
["Holy, Holy, Holy, Lord God Almighty"]

> Holy, holy, holy, Lord God Almighty,
>> who was, who is, who evermore shall be!
> Holy, holy, holy, Lord of heaven's army;
>> full of God's glory ever earth shall be!

Words of Institution

P: [Saint Paul writes:]
What I received from the Lord
I also hand down to you:

The Lord Jesus, in the night when he was betrayed,
took bread, and gave thanks,
broke it, and said,
"This is my body — on your behalf.
This do in remembrance of me."

Likewise also he took the cup —
after supper — and said,
"This cup is the new covenant in my blood.
This do, whenever you drink it, in remembrance of
me."

A: For whenever you eat this bread and drink the cup,
you proclaim the Lord's death until he comes.

C: **The cup of blessing which we bless,**
is it not a communion in the blood of Christ?
The bread that we break,
is it not a communion in the body of Christ?

A: For there is one bread;
and we are one body — though many members —
because we all share in the one bread.

C: **Amen.**

Lord's Prayer

Our Father in heaven,
 hallowed be your name,
 your kingdom come,
 your will be done,
 on earth as in heaven.
Give us today our daily bread.
Forgive us our sins
 as we forgive those
 who sin against us.
Save us from the time of trial
 and deliver us from evil.
For the kingdom, the power,
 and the glory are yours
 now and forever. Amen.

Invitation

A: Christ, our Passover Lamb,
  has been sacrificed on our behalf.
 Let us then celebrate the festival,
  not with the old leaven —
   the leaven of ill-will and evil —
 but with the unleavened bread
  of pure motives and truth.

C: Amen.

SIT

Distribution

[Congregational hymns, instrumental or vocal may be used during the distribution]

STAND

Pastoral Blessing

P: The body and blood of our Lord Jesus Christ
        keep you united to him,
            and with one another.

C: Amen.

Post-Communion Hymn

"Death Is Swallowed Up In Victory!"
Tune: *Old 124th,* 10 10 10 10 10
["Your Kingdom Come!"]

1.   Look! I will tell you a great mystery:
        we'll all be changed — not all of us will die —
     in the brief blinking of the human eye
        when the Last Trumpet summons us to God;
        a moment's time, and death will cease to be.

2.   The Trumpet peals; the dead in Christ arise;
        and we are changed — and we will never die!
     This mortal body, subject now to death,
        must put on that which never, ever dies —
        will put on that which never, ever dies!

3.   When this great transformation that we sing
        takes place, the Scriptures then will be fulfilled:
     "Death has been swallowed up in victory!
        Where then, O Death, is now your victory?
        Where, then, O Death, is now your deadly sting?"

SENDING

Exhortation

A: The sting of Death is Sin,
            and the power of Sin is the Law.

But thanks be to God
who gives us the victory
through Jesus Christ our Lord!
Therefore, beloved sisters and brothers,
be steadfast, immovable,
overflowing in the Lord's work all the time,
for you now realize that your work in the Lord
is never in vain.

C: Thanks be to God!

or

Doxology

P: The grace of the Lord Jesus Christ,
the love of God,
and the communion of the Holy Spirit
be with you all.

C: Amen.

Hymn

"Christ Is Risen!"
Tune: *Eden Church,* 87 87 87
["Christ Is Made The Sure Foundation"]

1. Just as through a human being,
   Death came in with all its dread,
   likewise through a Human Being
   came the Rising from the dead!
   Christ is risen, really risen,
   first-fruits from Death's earthen bed.

2. At Christ's coming — when the End comes —
   Christ will conquer'd Pow'rs unseat;
   Christ will place the Kingdom's Lordship
   in the Father's hands, complete!
   Christ must rule until God places
   all the Pow'rs beneath his feet.

3. All will then to Christ be subject —
   Rulers, Pow'rs, authority;
   when all things are subject to him,
   Christ to God will subject be:
   God will then be all in all things,
   and God's Kingdom we will see!

4. This the hope of Adam's children,
   that with Christ this song we sing:
   "Death is swallow'd up in vict'ry!"
   (Harrowed hell, your death-knell ring.)
   "Where, O Death, is now your vict'ry?
   Where, O Death, is now your sting?"

Sources for
"One Lord, One Body"
The Liturgical Witness Of
The Corinthian Letters

Hymn: 2 Corinthians 5:14-19
Pastoral Greeting: 1 Corinthians 1:3
Dialogue: 1 Corinthians 13 (NRSV)
Reading before the Psalm: 1 Corinthians 14:26 (NRSV)
Reading before the Second Lesson: 1 Corinthians 12:12-13
Reading before the Gospel Lesson: 1 Corinthians 1:18
Confession of Faith: 1 Corinthians 15:1-5; 1 Corinthians 8:6
Nicene Creed: International Consultation on English Texts
Offertory Canticle: 2 Corinthians 8:9; 9:7, 15
Great Thanksgiving: International Consultation on English Texts
Preface: 2 Corinthians 4:6 **or** 1 Corinthians 10:1-5
Holy, holy, holy: Revelation 4:8 and Isaiah 6:3
Words of Institution: 1 Corinthians 11:23-26; 1 Corinthians 10:16-17
Lord's Prayer: International Consultation on English Texts
Invitation: 1 Corinthians 5:7-8
Post-Communion Hymn: 1 Corinthians 5:51-58
Doxology: 2 Corinthians 13:14
Hymn: 1 Corinthians 15:20-26, 54-55

Unless otherwise noted, all translations, paraphrases, and versifications from
   the Greek New Testament are by Charles M. Mountain.

5

The Liturgical Witness Of Ephesians
[Epiphany, ABC; Ascension, ABC; Propers 10-16, B]

"One God And Father Of Us All"

Service of Holy Communion

GATHERING

[Prelude]

STAND

Processional Hymn

"Blesséd Be The God And Father"
Tune: *Hyfrydol,* 87 87 D
["Love Divine, All Loves Excelling"]

1. Blesséd be the God and Father,
        God of our Lord Jesus Christ!
    God in Christ blest us with blessings,
        spiritual wealth yet to be priced:
    God elected us in Jesus
        'fore the founding of the world!
    In God's eyes both whole and holy,
        we are loved before earth whirled.

2. God, in love, had long since planned it:
     our adoption as God's own.
   As God's children we were destined;
     and, through Christ, God made it known.
   God to us gave full redemption,
     sins' forgiveness through His blood,
   set us free from sin's enslavement,
     drowning death in Life's full flood.

3. This the plan that God intended
     for the Fullness of the Times:
   in Christ Jesus summing all things
     on the earth, in heav'nly climes.
   In Christ we obtained a birthright,
     that we may no more despair;
   Christ was made our elder brother,
     and, in him, all we are heir.

Pastoral Greeting

P: Grace to you, and peace,
     from God our Father,
     and Jesus Christ, our Lord.

C: Amen.

Confession of Faith

[Use either this creed reconstructed from Ephesians/Colossians, or the Nicene Creed below]

THE COLOSSIAN/EPHESIAN CREED

**We believe in God the Father,
   who gave us an inheritance
     among all God's people in the light;
   God rescued us from the tyranny of darkness,
     and returned us to the kingdom of God's Beloved Son,
   in whom we have redemption,
     the release, the forgiveness of sins.**

We believe in Jesus Christ,
   who is the image of the invisible God,
      the Lord of creation;
   who is also the beginning of the New Humanity,
      who is the Lord of death.
   For in Christ all the fulness of God dwells,
      and through Christ, God reconciled everything,
         making peace through Christ's death on the cross.
   Then God raised Christ from the dead,
      and gave to him all authority —
      not only in this Age,
         but also in the Age to come —
      placing all things under his feet.

We believe in the Holy Spirit,
   the down payment
      and assurance of our salvation,
   who unites us to Christ,
      and to all those who are his,
   who empowers us to live a life
      worthy of our Lord.

We believe that there is:
   one Body,
      and one Spirit,
         and one hope;
   one Lord,
      one faith,
         one Baptism;
   one God and Father of us all,
    who is above all,
      and through all,
         and in all. Amen.

or

NICENE CREED

We believe in one God,
   the Father, the Almighty,

maker of heaven and earth,
of all that is, seen and unseen.

We believe in one Lord, Jesus Christ,
the only Son of God,
eternally begotten of the Father,
God from God, Light from light,
true God from true God,
begotten, not made,
of one Being with the Father.
Through him all things were made.
For us and for our salvation
he came down from heaven;
by the power of the Holy Spirit
he became incarnate from the virgin Mary, and was made
man.
For our sake he was crucified under Pontius Pilate;
he suffered death and was buried.
On the third day he rose again
in accordance with the Scriptures;
he ascended into heaven
and is seated at the right hand of the Father.
He will come again in glory to judge the living and the dead,
and his kingdom will have no end.

We believe in the Holy Spirit, the Lord, the giver of life,
who proceeds from the Father and the Son.
With the Father and the Son he is worshiped and glorified.
He has spoken through the prophets.
We believe in one holy catholic and apostolic Church.
We acknowledge one Baptism for the forgiveness of sins.
We look for the resurrection of the dead,
and the life of the world to come. Amen.

Prayers

A: Let us pray.

[To these prayers may be added or substituted other petitions]

A: Father in heaven, God of our Lord Jesus Christ, give us the wisdom only you can give. Reveal your Beloved Son to everyone worshipping here, and to all your people throughout your worldwide Church. Give us the grace to truly know Jesus Christ as our Savior from sin and death, and as the only one through whom we are fully reconciled to you.

C: **Amen.**

A : We pray also, dear Father, that you will open our eyes and give us insight into the sure and certain hope to which you have called us, a hope based on the life, death, and resurrection of Jesus Christ, our Lord. Deliver us from the despair, the cynicism, and the other great and shameful sins which hold our unbelieving Age captive — and which so often bind us as well.

C: **Hear our prayer.**

A: Show us the riches of your inheritance in all the Christians of the world. We thank you that you have shown yourself as our Father and their Father, as our God and their God. Your work of reconciliation in Jesus' cross not only connects heaven and earth, but also all the members of Christ's body, the church.

C: **Amen.**

A: We pray also, Father, for the power which you unleashed through the resurrection of Christ, the power which overcame even death and sin, and enabled us to be raised up with Christ to your right hand. Let us see that power manifested among us by faith toward Jesus Christ, and by love for one another.

C: **Hear our prayer.**

SIT

WORD

Scripture Readings

First Lesson

[Said before the singing of the psalm of the day]

A: Keep yourselves under the influence of the Spirit
by addressing each other with spiritual
hymns, songs, and psalms from the heart to the
Lord,
constantly giving thanks at all times, and for the sake
of all,
in the Name of the Lord Jesus Christ
to God the Father.

Psalm

Second Lesson

STAND

Gradual

Tune: *Truro,* LM
["Christ Is Alive, Let Christians Sing"]

Sleeper, awake, rise from the dead,
and Christ, the Lord, will give you Light!
The Sun of Resurrection-pow'r,
Christ's rays will give you Light and Life!

Gospel Lesson

SIT

74

Hymn of the Day

"Christ The Victor Breached All Barriers"
Tune: *Hyfrydol,* 87 87 D
["Love Divine, All Loves Excelling"]

1.　Christ the Victor breached all barriers
　　　in his fight to set us free,
　　knocking down the best defenses
　　　of the ancient enmity:
　　walls of words, and bars of bias,
　　　fences formed from fear's finesse.
　　Ev'ry wall fell flat as Jéricho's,
　　　pulverized by love's largess.

2.　Nailed above the head of Jesus,
　　　there the barrier, Law, we see,
　　dying with him on the crossbeam
　　　with its legal enmity.
　　Christ, by taking all the hatred
　　　all the human race could mete,
　　turned our mutual hatred on us —
　　　made us one in love's defeat!

3.　Christ the Victor took them captive,
　　　all our ancient enmities,
　　race, religion, wealth and status —
　　　all lie shattered at his knees!
　　Christ then led them, shamed and broken,
　　　to his cross, where hatreds cease;
　　reconciled to one another,
　　　we are one in Christ, our peace.

Sermon

Offering
[An anthem, solo, or other music is appropriate here]

STAND

75

Offertory

"God's Gifts Are All We Have"
Tune: *Heath,* or any SM
["We Give Thee But Thine Own"]

1. God's gifts are all we have
      to offer God in praise;
    God's grace is all we have to claim
      when hearts to heav'n we raise.

2. Grace moved our God to save,
      to rescue us from sin;
    grace moved our God, no work of ours —
      not outward, nor within.

3. By grace we have been saved;
      our faith on God depends;
    by grace we work the works we do;
      grace guides us to God's ends.

[If Communion is not celebrated, worship continues with the Exhortation (Doxology) below]

[The ministers prepare the bread and wine for distribution]

MEAL

Words of Institution

P: In the night in which he was betrayed,
    our Lord Jesus took bread and gave thanks;
    broke it, and gave it to his disciples, saying,
    "Take and eat; this is my body, given for you.

    Do this for the remembrance of me."

    Again, after supper,
    he took the cup, gave thanks

and gave it for all to drink, saying,
"This cup is the new covenant in my blood,
shed for you and for all people
for the forgiveness of sins.

Do this for the remembrance of me."

Our Father in heaven
hallowed be your name,
your kingdom come,
your will be done,
on earth as in heaven.
Give us today our daily bread.
Forgive us our sins
as we forgive those
who sin against us.
Save us from the time of trial
and deliver us from evil.
For the kingdom, the power,
and the glory are yours
now and forever. Amen.

P: The peace of the Lord be with you now and always.

C: **And with you also.**

Sharing of the Peace

SIT

Distribution
[During the Distribution hymns and other music are appropriate]

STAND

Pastoral Blessing

P The Body and Blood of our Lord Jesus Christ
keep you united with him
and with one another.

C: **Amen.**

Post-Communion Prayer

A: Let us pray:

Give us, dear Father, according to the riches of your glory,
the strength which only you can give to our innermost
being.

Continue to dwell in us, O Christ, through faith,
and keep us grounded in your love.

Give us especially, Holy Spirit,
the power to fully understand with every Christian,
what is the breadth and length,
and the height and depth
of Christ's love for us —
a love beyond human understanding —
so that we may be filled with all the fulness of God.

C: **Amen.**

Words of Assurance

A: Remember:
You are no longer strangers and alien residents,
but you are fellow citizens with all of God's people;
you are also a part of God's household,
a household founded on the apostles and prophets,
with Jesus Christ as its chief cornerstone.

C: **Amen.**

SENDING

Doxology

P: Now to the One — who by the power at work among us
is able to accomplish infinitely more than we can ask
or imagine —
to God be the glory in the church and in Christ Jesus
throughout all the coming Ages.

C: **Amen.**

Hymn

"God Has Our Christ Raised Up"
Tune: *King's Weston,* 65 65 D
["At The Name Of Jesus"]

1. God has our Christ raised up,
     raised up from the dead;
   at God's right hand sat him,
     Lord of pow'rs we dread,
   far above all rulers,
     and the fame they claim,
   far above dominions,
     ev'ry name that's named.

2. Christ is Lord in this Age —
     and the Age to come!
   God put all things 'neath him;
     of all he's the sum.
   He's the church's heartbeat,
     breath and wherewithal,
   Head of God's own Body
     filling all in all!

Sources for
"One God And Father Of Us All"
The Liturgical Witness Of Ephesians

Processional Hymn: Ephesians 1:3-14
Pastoral Greeting: Ephesians 1:2
Confession of Faith: Colossians 1:12-15, 18-20; Ephesians 1:20-23; 4:4
Nicene Creed: International Consultation on English Texts
Prayers: Ephesians 1:15-20; Colossians 3:4
Reading before the Psalm: Ephesians 5:18-20
Gradual: Ephesians 5:14 and Clement of Alexandria, *Protepticus IX*
Sermon Hymn: Ephesians 2:14-16
Offertory: Ephesians 2:8-10
Lord's Prayer: International Consultation on English Texts
Post-Communion Prayer: Ephesians 3:14-19
Words of Assurance: Ephesians 2:19-22
Doxology: Ephesians 3:20-21
Hymn: Ephesians 1:20-23

Unless otherwise noted, all translations, paraphrases, and versifications from the Greek New Testament are by Charles M. Mountain.

6

The Liturgical Witness Of Philippians
[Advent 2-3, C; Holy Name, ABC; Palm/Passion Sunday, ABC; Propers 20-23, A]

"Always In The Lord Rejoice!"

GATHERING

[Prelude]

STAND

Entrance Hymn

"God In Form And God In Power"
Tune: *Hyfrydol,* 87 87 D
["Love Divine, All Loves Excelling"]

1. God in form and God in power,
        God in all equality,
    Christ the Lord became our servant,
        emptied, bound, to set us free!
    Christ was found in human semblance;
        lowly, he renounced his fame;
    to the point of death obedient,
        e'en a death by cross and shame.

2. Therefore God exalted Jesus,
    far above each counter-claim,
   with a Name above all others —
    all must kneel at Jesus' Name.
   Let the heavn'ns and all beneath them
    "Christ is Lord!" confession raise;
   tongues to Christ commence their chanting,
    to the Father's glory, praise!

Greeting

L: Grace to you, and peace, from God our Father, and the Lord Jesus Christ.

C: **And also to you.**

L: Let us pray:

Heavenly Father, we ask that our love for you and for our siblings in Christ would grow day by day. We also pray for the knowledge and enlightenment that we need to discern the things which are best for us and our neighbor. In the Day of Christ's return we ask to be pure and blameless, still eager to bring forth an abundant harvest of good deeds.

To you, most holy Father, be the glory and the praise, now and forever.

C: **Amen.**

Words of Assurance

L: Rest assured, brothers and sisters, that God, who began a good work in you, will continue that work until the Day of Jesus Christ.

C: **Amen.**

SIT

WORD

Scripture Readings

First Lesson

[Read after the First Lesson]

Let the way you live be worthy of the gospel of Christ.

Music
[An anthem, song, or other music is appropriate here]

Second Lesson

[Read after the Second Lesson]

You shine as lights in the world: hold fast the word of life.

Hymn of the Day

Sermon

STAND

Confession of Faith

APOSTLES' CREED

**I believe in God, the Father almighty,
creator of heaven and earth.**

**I believe in Jesus Christ, his only Son, our Lord,
He was conceived by the power of the Holy Spirit
and born of the virgin Mary.
He suffered under Pontius Pilate,
was crucified, died, and was buried.
He descended into hell.***

On the third day he rose again.
He ascended into heaven,
    and is seated at the right hand of the Father.
He will come again to judge the living and the dead.

I believe in the Holy Spirit, the holy catholic Church,
    the communion of saints,
    the forgiveness of sins,
    and resurrection of the body,
    and the life everlasting. Amen.

*Or, *He descended to the dead.*

L: Therefore, my sisters and brothers —
        loved and longed for,
            God's joy and crown —
        in this way stand firm in the Lord,
            for you are most belov'd.

C: **Amen.**

SIT

Offering

[An anthem, solo or other music is appropriate here]

STAND

Offertory Hymn

"Accept The Gifts We Bring"
Tune: *St. Thomas,* SM
["I Love Thy Kingdom, Lord"]

1.   Accept the gifts we bring,
        the tokens of your love
    that cancelled our compounded debt
        through Christ, sent from above.

2. And God, we know, fulfills
   our urgent, pressing needs
   according to the riches God,
   for Christ's sake, still us cedes.

3. Now to our Father, God,
   who blesses us with peace,
   be glory on the earth, in heav'n;
   let praises never cease!

[As the gifts are placed on the altar, the worship leader shall say:]

L: Saint Paul assures us:

I have learned,
   in whatever circumstances I find myself,
      to be content:
I know how to be humbled,
   I know how to abound;
in everything, I have learned the secret
   of being filled and of being hungry;
      of abundance and of want —
I can do all things
   in Christ who strengthens me!

C: Amen. Father, grant to us this same unwavering hope.

Prayers

L: Let us pray.

L: We pray first of all, our heavenly Father, that our fellowship would be one of encouragement in Christ, of love that comforts and gives renewed hope, of unity in the Spirit, of heartfelt affection and compassion toward one another — and of joy. We ask for the harmony which comes from similar goals, and the love which enables those goals to be met in peace.
Lord, in your mercy,

C: Hear our prayer.

L: Dear Father, we ask that in every way Christ be proclaimed to the world — starting from this place — and that more and more people know the joy and freedom of salvation. And if opposition should arise on account of the Word, enable us to remember that it is our privilege not only to believe in Christ, but, if necessary, also to suffer for his sake.
Lord, in your mercy,

C: **Hear our prayer.**

L: Father, enable us to be free of selfish ambition and empty self-glorification, but to consider others as more important than ourselves. Help us to be concerned — in a healthy, helpful way — with the needs and hopes of our sisters and brothers, and to help them bear their intolerable burdens.
Lord, in your mercy,

C: **Hear our prayer.**

[At this point may be added other petitions and thanksgivings]

L: Therefore, beloved of God, with fear and trembling let each of you work out his or her own salvation. For God is the one working within and among you, both to will and to work toward what pleases God.

C: **Amen.**

Lord's Prayer

Our Father in heaven,
hallowed be your name,
your kingdom come,
your will be done,
on earth as in heaven.
Give us today our daily bread.
Forgive us our sins
as we forgive those
who sin against us.

Save us from the time of trial
and deliver us from evil.
For the kingdom, the power,
and the glory are yours
now and forever. Amen.

Sharing of the Peace

Canticle

"Always In The Lord Rejoice"
Tune: *Gott sei Dank,* 77 77
["Spread, O Spread, Thou Mighty Word"]

1. Always in the Lord rejoice;
   and I say again, rejoice!
   let all your forbearance know,
   for the Lord is close, at hand.

2. Be not anxious for a thing,
   but in ev'rything by prayer
   and petition, giving thanks,
   your requests make known to God:

3. And the wondrous peace of God,
   far surpassing mind or thought,
   will stand guard around your hearts,
   and your minds, in Jesus Christ.

SENDING

Word of Peace

L: Finally, my friends:

Whatever is true, whatever is noble,
whatever is lovely, whatever is gracious,
if there is anything worthy of note and recognition —
set your mind on these things.
What you have learned
and received
and heard

and seen
in the spiritually mature, *do* —
and the God of peace will be with you.

C: Amen.

Hymn

"Here We Exist As Exiles Far From Home"
Tune: *Engelberg,* 10 10 10 4
["We Know That Christ Has Died"]

1.   Here we exist as exiles far from home;
        our heart and hearth are there, in heav'n above,
            while we await for Christ's return in love!
            Alleluia!

2.   For by the pow'r that subjects all to Christ,
        he'll change our lowly body that it be
            like his own ris'n and glorified body!
            Alleluia!

Sources for
"Always In The Lord Rejoice!"
The Liturgical Witness Of Philippians

Entrance Hymn: Philippians 2:6-11
Greeting: Philippians 1:2
Prayer: Philippians 1:9-11
Words of Assurance: Philippians 1:6
Reading after the First Lesson: Philippians 1:27
Reading after the Second Lesson: Philippians 2:15-16
Confession of Faith: International Consultation in English Texts
Exhortation: Philippians 4:1
Offertory Hymn: Philippians 4:18-20
Words of Assurance: Philippians 4:11-131
Prayers: Philippians 2:2, then 2:1; 1:18, 26; 2:3-13
Lord's Prayer: International Consultation on English Texts
Canticle: Philippians 4:4-7
Word of Peace: Philippians 4:8-9
Hymn: Philippians 3:20-21

Unless otherwise noted, all translations, paraphrases, and versifications from
the Greek New Testament are by Charles M. Mountain.

7

The Liturgical Witness Of Colossians
[Propers 10-13, C]

"Lordship And Unity"

Service of Holy Communion

GATHERING

[Prelude]

STAND

Processional Hymn

"Jesus Is The Image"
Tune: *King's Weston,* 65 65 D
["At The Name Of Jesus"]

1.   Jesus is the image
        of the God unseen;
     Lord of all creation,
        all that is, that's been.
     In Christ God created
        all that greets the eye —
     all things in the heavens;
        all beneath the sky.

2. In Christ God created
      things invisible —
   thrones, the lofty lordship,
      pow'rs, though Fall-able —
   all things God made through him;
      all for him was made.
   Christ gave them their power
      long 'fore light gave shade.

3. Christ was there beforehand,
      and God's plan helped trace;
   Christ holds all together;
      all in him has place.
   Christ is our life's pattern,
      first raised from the dead.
   First place our God gave him,
      making Christ the Head.

4. All the Deity's Fullness
      in Christ wished to dwell,
   all things reconciling,
      and our sin expel.
   God by reuniting
      through Christ's blood and cross —
   through Christ — earth and heaven,
      God restored our loss.

Pastoral Greeting

P: Grace to you, and peace,
   from God our Father.

C: **Amen.**

Dialogue

A: Let us give thanks to the Father,
C: **who enabled us to have our share
   in the inheritance with all the saints in the Light;**

who rescued us from the tyranny of Darkness,
   **and repatriated us into the Kingdom of God's Belovéd
      Son,**
in whom we have redemption:
   the release from, and the forgiveness of, sins.

Pastoral Assurance

P: In Christ, you who were at one time
      alienated and hostile in mind,
         doing evil things —
   you Christ has reconciled in his fleshly body
      through his death,
   in order to present you
      holy and blameless and without blemish
         before God.

C: Amen.

Confession of Faith

*[Use either this creed reconstructed from Ephesians/Colossians,
or the Nicene Creed below]*

THE COLOSSIAN/EPHESIAN CREED

We believe in God the Father,
   who gave us an inheritance
      among all God's people in the light;
   God rescued us from the tyranny of darkness,
      and returned us to the kingdom of God's Beloved Son,
   in whom we have redemption,
      the release, the forgiveness of sins.

We believe in Jesus Christ,
   who is the image of the invisible God,
      the Lord of creation;
   who is also the beginning of the New Humanity,
      who is the Lord of death.
   For in Christ all the fulness of God dwells,

and through Christ, God reconciled everything,
    making peace through Christ's death on the cross.
Then God raised Christ from the dead,
    and gave to him all authority —
    not only in this Age,
        but also in the Age to come —
    placing all things under his feet.

We believe in the Holy Spirit,
    the down payment
    and assurance of our salvation,
who unites us to Christ,
    and to all those who are his,
who empowers us to live a life
    worthy of our Lord.

For we believe that there is,
    one Body,
        and one Spirit,
        and one hope;
    one Lord,
        one faith,
        one Baptism;
    one God and Father of us all,
        who is above all,
        and through all,
            and in all. Amen.

                                    or

NICENE CREED

We believe in one God,
    the Father, the Almighty,
    maker of heaven and earth,
    of all that is, seen and unseen.

We believe in one Lord, Jesus Christ,
    the only Son of God,

eternally begotten of the Father,
God from God, Light from light,
true God from true God,
begotten, not made,
   of one Being with the Father.
   Through him all things were made.
   For us and for our salvation
      he came down from heaven;
      by the power of the Holy Spirit
      he became incarnate from the virgin Mary, and was made
         man.
   For our sake he was crucified under Pontius Pilate;
      he suffered death and was buried.
   On the third day he rose again
      in accordance with the Scriptures;
   he ascended into heaven
      and is seated at the right hand of the Father.
   He will come again in glory to judge the living and the dead,
      and his kingdom will have no end.

We believe in the Holy Spirit, the Lord, the giver of life,
   who proceeds from the Father and the Son.
   With the Father and the Son he is worshiped and glorified.
   He has spoken through the prophets.
   We believe in one holy catholic and apostolic Church.
      We acknowledge one Baptism for the forgiveness of sins.
We look for the resurrection of the dead,
      and the life of the world to come. Amen.

Prayers

A: Let us pray.

[To these prayers may be added or substituted other petitions]

A: Father in heaven, God of our Lord Jesus Christ, you have
    chosen us to be holy and beloved. Enable us to grow in
    compassion, kindness, lowliness, teachableness, and
    patience, that we may bear each other's faults as you

93

continue to bear ours. Enable us to always forgive each other as you in Christ have forgiven us.

C: **Amen.**

A: Father, above all enable us to put on love; for love binds all things together in perfect harmony.

C: **Amen.**

A: We always pray that the peace of God would rule as umpire in our hearts; for we were called into one body.

C: **Amen.**

A: We pray also, Father, that we would learn to become thankful.

C: **Amen.**

A: Give us all these things while we await with eager longing for the return in glory of Jesus Christ our Lord. For we believe the promise is also for us:
"When Christ, who is our life, is revealed,
then we also will be revealed with him in glory."

C: **Amen. Come soon, Lord Jesus.**

SIT

WORD

Scripture Readings

First Lesson

[Said before the singing of the psalm of the day]

A: Let the word of Christ dwell richly among you,
by teaching and encouraging each other in all wisdom;
and by singing psalms and hymns and spiritual songs
with thankfulness in your hearts to God.

Psalm

Second Lesson

[Said after the Second Lesson]

A: Whatever you do in word or deed,
      do it all in the name of the Lord Jesus,
         giving thanks to the Father through him.

STAND

Gospel Lesson

SIT

Hymn of the Day
[May be sung after the Sermon]

"O'er The Deadline Once Too Often"
Tune: *Hyfrydol,* 87 87 D
["Love Divine, All Loves Excelling"]

1.   O'er the deadline once too often
      we with free-bound feet trespassed.
   O'er we passed from Light to Darkness
      to the realm where Death speaks last,
   easy prey for human wisdom,
      and what passes for the Way,
   till Christ trespassed our trespasses,
      blinding Darkness with his Day!

2.   Nailed above the head of Jesus,
      dying with him on the tree,
   reads our record of indictments —
      ev'ry one a just decree.
   As Christ died to Law and judgment,
      so — joined with him — so did we;
   as Christ raised up serves God only,
      so we live in liberty!

3. Christ the Victor took them captive,
       all our ancient enemies,
   Sin and Law and Death and Satan,
       stripped their pow'r, their weapons seized.
   Christ then led them, shamed and broken,
       in his cross's triumph-parade;
   we're among the spoils he's taken,
       hope's freed pris'ners, unafraid.

Sermon

Offering

[An anthem, solo, or other music is appropriate here]

STAND

Offertory Hymn

"God's Gifts Are All We Have"
Tune: *Heath,* or any SM
["We Give Thee But Thine Own"]

1. God's gifts are all we have
       to offer God in praise;
   God's grace is all we have to claim
       when hearts to heav'n we raise.

2. Grace moved our God to save,
       to rescue us from sin;
   grace moved our God, no work of ours —
       not outward, nor within.

3. By grace we have been saved;
       our faith on God depends;
   by grace we work the works we do;
       grace guides us to God's end.

*[If Communion is **not** celebrated, worship continues with the Exhortation below]*

[The ministers prepare the bread and wine for distribution]

MEAL

Words of Institution

P: In the night in which he was betrayed,
our Lord Jesus took bread and gave thanks;
broke it, and gave it to his disciples, saying,
"Take and eat; this is my body, given for you.

Do this for the remembrance of me."

Again, after supper,
he took the cup, gave thanks
and gave it for all to drink, saying,
"This cup is the new covenant in my blood,
shed for you and for all people
for the forgiveness of sins.

Do this for the remembrance of me."

**Our Father in heaven
hallowed be your name,
your kingdom come,
your will be done,
on earth as in heaven.
Give us today our daily bread.
Forgive us our sins
as we forgive those
who sin against us.
Save us from the time of trial
and deliver us from evil.
For the kingdom, the power,
and the glory are yours
now and forever. Amen.**

P: The peace of the Lord be with you now and always.

C: **And with you also.**

Sharing of the Peace

SIT

Distribution

[During the distribution hymns and other music are appropriate]

STAND

Pastoral Blessing

P: The Body and the Blood of our Lord Jesus Christ
keep you united with him
and with one another.

C: Amen.

Word of Exhortation

A: Since you were raised up by God in Christ,
keep on seeking the things above,
where Christ is,
seated in the place of power
at God's right hand.
For you have died,
and your life, for now,
is hidden with Christ in God.
But when Christ — who is our life — is revealed,
then we will be revealed with him
in glory.

C: Amen.

SENDING

Doxology

P: The Lord bless you,
and keep you.

The Lord's face shine upon you,
  and be gracious to you.
The Lord's countenance be lifted upon you,
  and give you peace.

C: Amen.

Hymn

"The Universe Is Cruciform"
Tune: *Third Mode Melody,* CMD

1. The universe is cruciform,
      for Christ died on a Tree,
    and Christ's obedience upon death
      reversed life's entropy.
    Our woes arose in Adam's time,
      when he and Eve — still free —
    chose freely God to disobey,
      duped by the Enemy.

2. Then sin and death came rushing in
      to fill the God-void space,
    its height, its depth, its length and breadth,
      it's ev'ry time and place.
    With rod of iron these tyrants ruled
      o'er all the human race!
    Enslaved, ashamed, we hid from God,
      estranged from Life and grace.

3. But must sin's rule be absolute?
      Must death dog all our days?
    Must hopelessness and deep despair
      reign on while life decays?
    No! On the Cross, the ransom-price —
      Life's Lord — by death defrays,
    and now arisen from the dead,
      the death of death displays!

4. For Christ is God's almighty Word,
    pervading space and time,
   its height, its depth, its length and breadth —
    Creation's paradigm.
   In Christ all things have proper place;
    in all things, Christ is prime.
   For Christ is Head of heav'n and earth,
    or lowly or sublime.

5. The universe is cruciform;
    the Cross shall all unite.
   The Cross's depth imprints the earth,
    its height lights heaven bright;
   it lengthens long from East to West,
    its open arms invite
   those scattered wide to gather in
    from death's domain and night.

Sources for
"Lordship And Unity"
The Liturgical Witness Of Colossians

Processional Hymn: Colossians 1:14-20
Pastoral Greeting: Colossians 1:2
Dialogue: Colossians 1:12-14
Pastoral Assurance: Colossians 1:21-22
Confession of Faith: Colossians 1:12-15, 18-20; Ephesians 1:20-23; 4:4
Nicene Creed: International Consultation on English Texts
Prayers: Colossians 3:12-15; 3:4
Reading before the Psalm: Colossians 3:16
Reading after the Second Lesson: Colossians 3:17
Sermon Hymn: Colossians 2:13-15
Offertory Hymn: Ephesians 2:8-10
Words of Institution: International Consultation on English Texts
Lord's Prayer: International Consultation on English Texts
Word of Exhortation: Colossians 3:1-4
Doxology: Numbers 6:24-26
Hymn: Irenaeus, *Epideixis,* 34

Unless otherwise noted, all translations, paraphrases, and versifications from
    the Greek New Testament and Irenaeus are by Charles M. Mountain.

8

The Liturgical Witness Of The Thessalonian Letters

[Advent Season; Propers 24-28, A; Propers 26-28, C]

"The Day Of The Lord"

Service of Holy Communion

GATHERING

[Prelude]

STAND

Entrance Hymn

"We Grieve, But Not As Others"
Tune: *Aurelia,* 76 76 D
["The Church's One Foundation"]

1. We grieve, but not as others
        who do not hold our Hope;
    who unbelief has blinded —
        in death's despair they grope!
    For, as we trust that Jesus
        was dead and then arose,
    so God will bring, through Jesus,
        our dead, freed from death-throes.

2. For Christ himself, descending,
   will cry the great command;
and at the trumpet's fanfare,
   the dead in Christ will stand.
Then those alive are caught up
   to join the living cloud,
to be with Christ forever,
   released from death's tight shroud.

3. So comfort one another
   with this, our living Hope,
and let its expectation
   be seen in widest scope:
For whether dead, or living,
   we with our Lord will be,
from Sin and Satan's power,
   from Death's despair — set free!

Pastoral Greeting

P: Grace to you and peace
   from God our Father,
      and the Lord, Jesus Christ.

C: Amen.

Dialogue

A: As the lightning comes from the east
C: **and flashes as far as the west,**
so will be the coming
   of the Son of Man.
But on what day and hour
   no one knows,
neither heaven's angels, nor the Son,
   but the Father only.
Then two men will be at work;
   one will be taken and one will be left.

Then two women will be working together;
   one will be taken and one will be left.
Let us keep awake therefore,
   for we do not know
on what day, or at what hour,
   our Lord is coming.

Old Testament Canticle

"Is This The Day You Long And Pine For?"
Tune: *Wenn nur den lieben Gott,* 98 98 88
["If You But Suffer God To Guide Thee"]

1. Is this the Day you look and long for —
       God's coming Day — to set you free?
    Behold, the Day of God is darkness,
       shadows so thick, you cannot see.
    Is not this Day a night of glooms,
       since God's just judgment o'er you looms?

2. "Take from me — now — your noxious noises!
       Your empty songs of 'praise and joy.'
    'Full-fill' your psalms with deeds of mercy,
       then let your choral corps deploy:
    let justice roll, a flood supreme;
       right deeds, an ever-flowing stream!"

SIT

WORD

Scripture Readings
[Music is appropriate before or after any of the readings]

   First Lesson

   Psalm *[preferably sung]*

STAND

103

Gospel Lesson

SIT

<u>Hymn of the Day</u>

Sermon

STAND

<u>Confession of Faith</u>

APOSTLES' CREED

I believe in God, the Father almighty,
creator of heaven and earth.

I believe in Jesus Christ, his only Son, our Lord.
He was conceived by the power of the Holy Spirit
and born of the virgin Mary.
He suffered under Pontius Pilate,
was crucified, died, and was buried.
He descended into hell.*
On the third day he rose again.
He ascended into heaven,
and is seated at the right hand of the Father.
He will come again to judge the living and the dead.

I believe in the Holy Spirit, the holy catholic Church,
the communion of saints,
the forgiveness of sins,
the resurrection of the body,
and the life everlasting. Amen.

*Or, He descended to the dead.

SIT

Offering
[An anthem, solo, or other music is appropriate here]

STAND

104

Offertory Canticle

"We Are The Lord's"
Tune: *Duke Street,* LM
["Jesus Shall Reign Wherever The Sun"]

1. No one of us to herself lives;
        no one of us to himself dies.
    For, if we live, to Christ we live;
        and if we die, to Christ we die.

2. Whether we live, whether we die,
        we are the Lord's, of this be sure.
    For Christ once died, yet lives again;
        Christ is the Lord of Life and Death.

Prayers and the Sharing of the Peace

*[If Communion is **not** celebrated, the service continues with
the **Post-Communion Prayer**, below]*

[The ministers then prepare the bread and wine for distribution]

MEAL

Words of Institution

P: In the night in which he was betrayed,
    our Lord Jesus took bread and gave thanks;
    broke it, and gave it to his disciples, saying,
    "Take and eat; this is my body, given for you.

    Do this for the remembrance of me."

Again, after supper,
he took the cup, gave thanks
and gave it for all to drink, saying,
"This cup is the new covenant in my blood,
shed for you and for all people
for the forgiveness of sins.

Do this for the remembrance of me."

A: Whenever we eat this bread,
and drink from this cup,

C: **we recall our Lord's death
until he comes again.**

Lord's Prayer

A: Give to us now your Holy Spirit, O Lord,
that we may boldly, and from the heart,
invoke you as our Father
as we pray:

**Our Father in heaven
hallowed be your name,
your kingdom come,
your will be done,
on earth as in heaven.
Give us today our daily bread.
Forgive us our sins
as we forgive those
who sin against us.
Save us from the time of trial
and deliver us from evil.
For the kingdom, the power,
and the glory are yours
now and forever. Amen.**

SIT

Distribution

[Congregational hymns, instrumental or vocal music. Suggested hymns: "When Peace, Like A River," "Who Is This Host Arrayed In White?" "Oh, Happy Day When We Shall Stand," and the like]

STAND

Pastoral Blessing

P: And now may our Lord Jesus Christ,
    and God our Father —
        who loved us,
        and gave us eternal comfort
        and a sure and certain hope —
  encourage your hearts,
    and strengthen you
        in every good work and word.

C: **Amen.**

or

P: Now may the Lord of peace
    give you peace at all times
    and in every way.
  The Lord be with you all.

C: **Amen.**

Post-Communion Prayer

A: Let us pray:

A: Remember your church, O Lord:
    Rescue it from all evil,
        and bring it to maturity in your love;
    gather it from the four winds into your Kingdom,
        a Kingdom prepared for it before the beginning of
          time.

C: **For yours, O Lord, is the power and the glory forever. Amen.**

A: Our Lord, come; and this Age pass away!

C: **Amen. Come soon, Lord Jesus!**

Hosanna

Tune: *Gelobt sei Gott,* 888 with Alleluias
["Good Christians, Friends, Rejoice And Sing!"]

ALL: Hosanna to king David's son!
Bless'd is the one in God's name come!
Highest hosannas now be sung!
***O maran-atha, O maran-atha* — "O, our Lord, come!"**

Exhortation

A: Rejoice always,
pray without ceasing,
give thanks in all circumstances;
for this is the will of God
in Christ Jesus for you.

C: **Amen.**

SENDING

Benediction

P: And now may the God of peace
keep you whole and holy;
and may your spirit and soul and body
be blameless and at peace
at the coming of our Lord Jesus Christ.

Faithful is the One who calls you —
who also will do it.

C: Amen.

Hymn

"As For God's Times And Seasons"
Tune: *Aurelia,* 76 76 D
["The Church's One Foundation"]

1. As for God's times and seasons
       you need know nothing more,
    except our Lord's returning
       is soon — he's at the door!
    For like a thief at midnight
       who suddenly breaks in,
    Christ will — and unexpected —
       break through the night of sin.

2. The Day will soon be dawning,
       O Children of the Light!
    Let darkness' works be cast off,
       and sin's remaining blight,
    Yet we are not in darkness,
       O Children of the Day!
    Let's keep awake and watchful
       lest back to night we stray.

3. Yet we have not been chosen
       for wrath's rejecting word,
    but chosen for salvation
       through Jesus Christ, our Lord.
    God's Chosen, Christ, died for us;
       we, raised with Him, life see.
    So whether dead or living
       we with our Lord will be.

Sources for
"The Day Of The Lord"
The Liturgical Witness Of The Thessalonian Letters

Entrance Hymn: 1 Thessalonians 4:13-18; 5:10
Pastoral Greeting: 2 Thessalonians 1:2
Dialogue: Matthew 24:27, 40-42
Old Testament Canticle: Amos 5:18-24 (Old Testament Cant.)
Offertory Canticle: Romans 14:8-9
Words of Institution: International Consultation on English Texts
Words following: 1 Corinthians 11:26
Lord's Prayer: International Consultation on English Texts
Pastoral Blessing: 2 Thessalonians 2:16-17 **or** 2 Thessalonians 3:16
Post-Communion Prayer and Hosanna: *Didaché*, X:5-6
Benediction: 1 Thessalonians 5:23-24
Hymn: 1 Thessalonians 5:1-10

Unless otherwise acknowledged, all translations, paraphrases, and versifications from the Greek New Testament and the *Didaché* are by Charles M. Mountain.

9

The Liturgical Witness Of
The Pastoral Letters

*[Christmas Season; Epiphany Season, or
any time the theme is revelation; Propers 19-25, C]*

"The Saying Is Sure"

Service of Holy Communion

GATHERING

[Prelude]

STAND

<u>Entrance Hymn</u>

"The Grace Of Our Great Savior, God"
Tune: *Melita,* 88 88 88
["My Hope Is Built On Nothing Less"]

1. The grace of our great Savior, God,
    in our time was made manifest;
    and training us to purify
    our lives, grace guides us to God's best.
       Let sin, now pow'rless, rail and rage;
       we live to God — and in this Age!

2. Our blesséd hope we now await,
th'appearance soon and glorious
of our great God and Savior, Christ,
who gave himself for all of us.
Redeemed from sin, his folk are we,
who zealous for good works will be.

Pastoral Greeting

P: Grace, mercy, and peace to you
from God the Father
and Christ Jesus our Lord.

C: **And also to you.**

Hymn of Praise

"The Goodness And The Graciousness Of God"
Tune: *Vom Himmel hoch,* LM
["From Heaven Above To Earth I Come"]

1. The goodness and the graciousness
of God, our Savior, have appeared;
who saved us, not through our good works,
but by a grace that never veered!

2. God's means: the water with the word,
which give us new life through our Lord;
God's Spirit guides us, and makes new
God's Image lost, by Christ restored!

3. The living Spirit God poured out,
a flood of love beyond our prayers.
So we are justified by grace,
and life eternal's "hope-full" heirs!

Prayer of the Day

SIT

WORD

Scripture Readings

[Music is appropriate before or after any of the readings]

[Said before the First Lesson]

A: All Scripture is God-breathed,
     and is profitable for teaching,
      for restraining ungodly —
     and encouraging godly — behavior,
      as well as for training in what pleases God,
     so that the godly person might be complete,
      and ready for every good work.

First Lesson

Psalm *[preferably sung]*

Second Lesson

STAND

Gospel Lesson

SIT

Hymn of the Day

"God It Is Who Saved And Called Us"
Tune: *Praise, My Soul,* 87 87 87
["Praise, My Soul, The King Of Heaven"]

1.   God it is who saved and called us
     (time cannot this call efface),
   not through our weak works or efforts,
     but through God's great plan and grace,
   grace God gave us in Christ Jesus
     long before all time began.

2. With th'appearing of Christ Jesus,
   God's salvation manifest,
   who, through Christ's death, death abolish'd,
   blotting out death's last bequest.
   Life immortal through the Gospel! —
   now reveal'd as God's great plan.

Sermon

STAND

Confession of Faith
[The Apostles' or Nicene Creed may be used instead]
THE "PASTORAL" CREED

We believe in God the Father:
   creator of the heavens and the earth,
      the blessed and only Sovereign,
   the King of the Ages,
      immortal, invisible,
   the only, true, and living God,
      who dwells in unapproachable light,
         who is King of kings and Lord of lords.

We believe in Jesus Christ, our Lord,
   descended from David,
      who came into the world to save sinners.
   For there is only one Mediator
      between the one God and human beings,
         the human being, Christ Jesus,
            who gave himself a ransom for all;
               who God also raised from the dead.

We believe in the Holy Spirit:
   who dwells in our hearts
      and continues to renew us;
   and, since we are justified by grace,
      the Holy Spirit witnesses that we are heirs
         in the hope of eternal life;

114

who also makes of us together
the household and church of the living God.

We now await the blest hope,
the sudden appearance of the glory
of our great God and Savior, Jesus Christ;
who gave himself on our behalf,
not only to redeem us from all sin,
but also to purify for himself a people
zealous for good works. Amen.

or

APOSTLES' CREED

I believe in God, the Father almighty,
creator of heaven and earth.

I believe in Jesus Christ, his only Son, our Lord.
He was conceived by the power of the Holy Spirit
and born of the virgin Mary.
He suffered under Pontius Pilate,
was crucified, died, and was buried.
He descended into hell.*
On the third day he rose again.
He ascended into heaven,
and is seated at the right hand of the Father.
He will come again to judge the living and the dead.

I believe in the Holy Spirit, the holy catholic Church,
the communion of saints,
the forgiveness of sins,
the resurrection of the body,
and the life everlasting. Amen.

*Or, *He descended to the dead.*

SIT

Offering

[An anthem, solo, or other music is appropriate here]

A: We brought nothing into the world;
    and it is certain
        we cannot take anything out of the world;
    but if we have food and clothing,
        with these let us be content.

STAND

Offertory Canticle

"If We With Him Have Died"
Tune: *Rhosymedre,* 66 66 888
["My Song Is Love Unknown"]

    If we with him have died,
        then with him we will live.
    If we endure, we'll reign
        forever with him too.
    If we deny him, he'll d'ny us.
    If we are faithless, still he's true —
        for he cannot himself deny.

Offertory Prayer

A: Our Savior God,

C: **we give to you only what you have first given us. And we know that everything created by you is good, and that nothing is to be rejected if it is received with thanksgiving, for then it is set apart as holy by the word of God and prayer. Amen.**

Prayers

A: Let us remember that we are urged to make supplications, prayers, intercessions, and thanksgivings for all people, especially for political leaders and all who are in high position, that we may live our lives quietly and peaceably, godly and respectable in every way. This is good and acceptable in the sight of God our Savior, who desires all people to be saved and to come to the knowledge of the truth.

A: Let us pray:

[Here prayers for the world, local, state, and national governments, the worldwide, regional and local churches, as well as for the congregation's specific needs, may be said]

Sharing of the Peace

[The ministers then prepare the bread and wine for distribution]

MEAL

Great Thanksgiving

P: The Lord be with you.

C: And also with you.

P: Lift up your hearts.

C: We lift them up to the Lord.

P: Let us thank the Lord our God.

C: It is right to give God thanks and praise.

Preface

P: It is right that we praise and thank you, God our Father, for sending your love and mercy, especially the mercy shown to us in the sending of our Savior, Christ Jesus —

ALL: *[sung]*

Tune: *Nun danket alle Gott,* 67 67 66 66
["Now Thank We All Our God"]

> For there is but one God;
>   and one the Mediator
> 'tween humans and their God,
>   the human being, Jesus,
> who gave himself for all
>   the ransom for our sin;
> who at th'appointed time,
>   was sent to save us all.

or

P: It is right that we praise and thank you, God our Father, for your love and mercy, especially the mercy shown to us in the sending of our Savior, Christ Jesus —

> For God's firm foundation stands,
>   bearing this seal:
> *"The Lord knows his people";*
>   and,
> *"Let everyone who names the name of the Lord*
>   *forsake sinful behavior."*

[The following words always conclude the Preface, no matter which text above is chosen:]

P: And so with saints Paul and Timothy and Titus,
>   and with all your saints of all the Ages,
> we also confess that the mystery of our faith is great:
>   Namely, God who ...

ALL: *[sung]*

Tune: *Praise, My Soul,* 87 87 87
["Praise, My Soul, The King Of Heaven"]

> In the flesh was manifested;
>   in the Spirit justified.

By the angels was seen also,
   to the nations was proclaimed.
In the world was then believed on,
   and in glory taken up.

Words of Institution

P: In the night in which he was betrayed,
    our Lord Jesus took bread and gave thanks;
    broke it, and gave it to his disciples, saying,
    "Take and eat; this is my body, given for you.

    Do this for the remembrance of me."

    Again, after supper,
    he took the cup, gave thanks
    and gave it for all to drink, saying,
    "This cup is the new covenant in my blood,
    shed for you and for all people
    for the forgiveness of sins.

    Do this for the remembrance of me."

Our Father in heaven
   hallowed be your name,
   your kingdom come,
   your will be done,
   on earth as in heaven.
Give us today our daily bread.
Forgive us our sins
   as we forgive those
   who sin against us.
Save us from the time of trial
   and deliver us from evil.
For the kingdom, the power,
   and the glory are yours
   now and forever. Amen.

SIT

Distribution

[Hymns, instrumental, or vocal music may be used during the distribution]

STAND

Pastoral Blessing

P: May the Body and Blood of our Lord Jesus Christ strengthen you and keep you in his grace.

C: Amen.

SENDING

Doxology

P: And now to the King of the Ages —
immortal, invisible,
the only God —
be honor and glory
forever and ever!

C: Amen.

Hymn

Sources for
"The Saying Is Sure"
The Liturgical Witness of The Pastoral Letters

Entrance Hymn: Titus 2:11-14
Pastoral Greeting: 1 Timothy 1:2
Hymn of Praise: Titus 3:4-8
Reading before the First Lesson: 2 Timothy 3:16-17
Creed: composite of words from the confessional statements in the Pastorals
Apostles' Creed: International Consultation on English Texts
Sermon Hymn: 2 Timothy 1:9-10
Reading before the Offering is received: 1 Timothy 6:7-8
Offertory Canticle: 2 Timothy 2:12-13
Offertory Prayer: 1 Timothy 4:4-5
Prayers: 1 Timothy 2:1-4 (RSV)
Prefaces: 1 Timothy 2:5-6; 2 Timothy 2:19; 1 Timothy 3:16
Lord's Prayer: International Consultation on English Texts
Doxology: 1 Timothy 1:1-17

Unless otherwise noted, all translations, paraphrases, and versifications from
the Greek New Testament are by Charles M. Mountain.

10

The Liturgical Witness Of Hebrews

[Propers 22-28, B; Propers 14-17, C;
Annunciation, ABC; Presentation, ABC;
Good Friday, ABC]

"Prophet, Priest, And King"

Service of Holy Communion

GATHERING

[Prelude]

STAND

Entrance Hymn

"In Many And Various Ways Of Old"
Tune: *Den signede Dag,* 98 98 98
["O Day Full Of Grace"]

1.   In many and various ways of old
God spoke to us through the prophets;
but in these Last Days, just as foretold,
to us, through a Son, God's spoken,
    installed by God heir of ev'rything;
    through whom are the Ages springing.

2. Christ beams with effulgent rainbow light,
   and bears the stamp of God's being;
   Christ's word all maintains by might of right;
   for sin made the greater Cleansing;
   Christ rules through God's own great Majesty
   with God in God's endless glory!

Dialogue

A: Christ is far superior to angels
C: **because Christ inherited a much more excellent name than theirs.**
For to which angel did God ever say,
"You are my Son; today I have begotten you"?
And, "In the beginning, Lord, you established the earth,
and the heavens are the work of your hands;
They will perish,
but you forever remain;
They will all wear out like clothing;
like a cloak you will roll them up,
and like clothing they will be changed —
but you are the same, and your years will never end."
And to which of the angels did God ever say,
"Sit at my right hand until I make your enemies a footstool for your feet"?
Therefore, let us pay even greater attention to the Good News we have heard,
lest we drift away from it, like a ship without an anchor.

SIT

WORD

Scripture Readings

[Music is appropriate before or after any of the readings]

[Said before the First Lesson]

The word of God is living and active, sharper than any two-edged sword, piercing until it divides soul from spirit, joints from marrow; it is able to judge the thoughts and intentions of the heart. Before God no creature is hidden, but all are naked and laid bare to the eyes of the one to whom we must render an account.

First Lesson *[Frequent use of Jeremiah 31:31-34 is urged]*

Psalm *[Always Psalm 8, preferably sung]*

[Sung after the Psalm]

Hymn Response to Psalm 8

"But We See Jesus"
Tune: *Old 124th,* 10 10 10 10 10
["Thy Kingdom Come"]

1. We do not see "all things beneath his feet";
       but we see Jesus, "for a time made low";
   "Crowned" now "with glory and with honor,"
       since he endured the suffering of death,
           that by God's grace might taste of and death know.

2. For God, for whom and by whom all exists,
       salvation's Pioneer made — by great shame —
   precisely by his suffering, mature!
       So, Christ, the Sanctifier — and we too,
           those sanctified by him — one Father name!

Second Lesson

[Said after the Second Lesson]

Now faith is the assurance of things hoped for,
    the conviction of things not seen.

STAND

Gospel Lesson

[Said after the Gospel Lesson]

Jesus Christ is the same, yesterday, today, and forever.

SIT

Hymn of the Day

"For Since The Children Share In Flesh And Blood"
Tune *Melita,* 88 88 88
["Eternal Father, Strong To Save"]

1. For, since the children share in flesh
and blood, Christ shared himself the same,
that through his death he might destroy
the one who pow'r of death could claim,
and free those who through fear of death
were Satan's slaves with ev'ry breath.

2. For Christ was obligated, like
his siblings, to be flesh and bone,
to be a High Priest merciful,
and for his people's sins atone.
Thus like his suff'ring people made,
he's always willing to give aid.

Sermon

STAND

Confession of Faith
[The Nicene Creed may be said on Festival Days]

APOSTLES' CREED

**I believe in God, the Father almighty,
creator of heaven and earth.**

I believe in Jesus Christ, his only Son, our Lord.
   He was conceived by the power of the Holy Spirit
      and born of the virgin Mary.
   He suffered under Pontius Pilate,
      was crucified, died, and was buried.
   He descended into hell.*
   On the third day he rose again.
   He ascended into heaven,
      and is seated at the right hand of the Father.
   He will come again to judge the living and the dead.

I believe in the Holy Spirit, the holy catholic Church,
   the communion of saints,
   the forgiveness of sins,
   the resurrection of the body,
   and the life everlasting. Amen.

*Or, *He descended to the dead.*

SIT

Offering

[An anthem, solo, or other music is appropriate here]

STAND

Offertory

"Grace And Timely Help"
Tune: *Gott sei Dank,* 77 77
["Spread, O Spread, Thou Mighty Word"]

1.   Jesus Christ, the Son of God,
         is our High and Faithful Priest,
      who went 'fore us through the heav'ns;
         there his prayers have never ceased!

2.   For our High Priest really is
         sympathetic to our plight;
      like us — though he never sinned —
         he was tested in the fight.

3. Let us then with confidence
      to the throne of grace draw near,
   that we mercy may receive,
      grace and help in time of fear.

Prayers

Lord's Prayer

**Our Father in heaven,
hallowed be your name,
your kingdom come,
your will be done,
on earth as in heaven.
Give us today our daily bread.
Forgive us our sins
as we forgive those
who sin against us.
Save us from the time of trial
and deliver us from evil.
For the kingdom, the power,
and the glory are yours
now and forever. Amen.**

Sharing of the Peace

[The ministers then prepare the bread and wine for distribution]

SIT

MEAL

Thanksgiving

P: To you, heavenly Father, be all the thanks and praise,
for in our Lord Christ — once for all offered up —
you have provided for us the perfect sacrifice for sin.

For Christ has appeared once for all
　　at the consummation of the Age
　　　　in order to remove sin by the sacrifice of himself.
And just as it is appointed for people to die once,
　　and after that the judgment,
so Christ, who was offered once to bear the sins of many,
　　will be seen a second time, not to deal with sin,
　　　　but to save those who are eagerly waiting for him.

C: **Amen. We await your coming, Lord.**
　　　Come soon, and save us to the uttermost.

P: For Christ, after offering for all time
　　a single sacrifice for sins,
　　　　"sat down at the right hand of God";
and since then has been waiting
　　"until his enemies are a footstool for his feet."
For by a single offering
　　he has perfected forever those who are sanctified.

C: **Amen. Christ the Victor, Christ the Victim;**
　　　Christ the Victim, Christ the Priest.

Words of Institution

P: In the night in which he was betrayed,
　　our Lord Jesus took bread and gave thanks;
　　broke it, and gave it to his disciples, saying,
　　"Take and eat; this is my body, given for you.

Do this for the remembrance of me."

Again, after supper,
he took the cup, gave thanks
and gave it for all to drink, saying,
"This cup is the new covenant in my blood,
shed for you and for all people
for the forgiveness of sins.

Do this for the remembrance of me."

129

A: For, after coming into the world, Christ said:
"Sacrifices and offerings you did not want,
but a body you have prepared for me;
burnt offerings and sin offerings
are not well-pleasing to you."
Then he said,
"Behold, I have come to do your will, O God."
And it is by God's will
that we have been sanctified
through the offering of the body
of Jesus Christ once for all.

C: **Amen. Christ is God's Lamb,
bearing away the sin of the world.**

A: Let us then approach God with a true heart
in full assurance of faith;
let us hold fast to the confession of our hope,
for God, who has promised, is faithful.

Canticle Response

"Salvation's Source"
Tune: *Olivet,* 664 66 64
["My Faith Looks Up To Thee"]

1. Christ, in his days of flesh,
offer'd, with cries and tears,
prayers up to God.
Christ, filled with death-dread fears,
prayed, "My God, rescue me!" —
and, for his godliness,
God heard his Word!

2. For, though Christ is God's Son,
he learned obedience
by suffering.
And, made mature, Christ is
salvation's sustenance
for all who hear the Word,
who lean on God.

130

Distribution

[Congregational hymns, instrumental or vocal music may be used during the distribution. The following hymn may be sung or any other appropriate hymn]

STAND

Post-Communion Hymn

"When God Desired To Show"
Tune: *Lobe den Herren,* 14 14 478
["Praise To The Lord, The Almighty, The King Of Creation"]

1. When God desired to show heirs of the long-waited promise
    just how unchangeable was the intent of His purpose,
    God interposed,
    swearing by Himself an oath
    (swearing to others is pointless).

2. So then, by two facts unchangeable — God's oath and promise —
    we who for refuge have fled might take courage and prowess
    to seize the hope
    before us set as our goal —
    God will not lie nor hold malice.

3. This hope we have for our soul as a sure, steady anchor —
    this hope that's moored in God's presence there, beyond all censure,
    where Jesus went,
    forerunner on our behalf —
    he is our High Priest forever!

Pastoral Blessing

P: And now may the body and blood
offered up for us once for all,
assure you of the complete forgiveness
of all your sins:
For Christ is able for all time to save completely
all who approach God through him,
since he always lives
to intercede for them.

C: Amen.

SENDING

Benediction

P: Now may the God of peace —
who brought up from the dead our Lord Jesus,
the Great Shepherd of the sheep —
by the blood of the eternal covenant,
make you complete in everything good
so that you may do God's will,
working among you
that which is pleasing in God's sight,
through Jesus Christ,
to whom be the glory forever and ever.

C: Amen.

Hymn

"Christ Has Appeared"
Tune: *Engelberg,* 10 10 10 with Alleluia
["We Know That Christ Has Died"]

1.   Christ has appeared so near this Age's End
to make himself an off'ring for our sin;
that he the barrier to our God might rend!
Alleluia!

2. Christ entered in the holy place above
   with his own blood, th'atoning sacrifice;
   he there appears to plead for us in love.
   Alleluia!

3. Christ will on earth a second time appear —
   though not to deal with sin and death's dread fear —
   to save us eagerly who 'wait him here!
   Alleluia!

Sources for
"Prophet, Priest, And King"
The Liturgical Witness of Hebrews

Entrance Hymn: Hebrews 1:1-4
Dialogue: Hebrews 1:5-13
Reading before the First Lesson: Hebrews 4:12-13
Hymn Response to the Psalm: Hebrews 2:8-11
Reading after the Second Lesson: Hebrews 11:1
Reading after the Gospel Lesson: Hebrews 13:8
Offertory: Hebrews 4:14-16
Lord's Prayer: International Consultation on English Texts
Words surrounding the Words of Institution: Hebrews 9:26-28; 10:12-14;
    10:5-7, 10
Words of Institution: International Consultation on English Texts
Canticle Response: Hebrews 5:7-9
Pastoral Blessing: Hebrews 7:25 (NRSV, altered slightly)
Benediction: Hebrews 13:20-21
Hymn: Hebrews 9:26-28

Unless otherwise acknowledged, all translations, paraphrases, and versifi-
    cations from the Greek New Testament are by Charles M. Mountain.

11

The Liturgical Witness Of First Peter
[Easter 2-7, A]

"A Living Hope"

Service of Holy Communion

GATHERING

[Prelude]

STAND

<u>Entrance Hymn</u>

"Blesséd Be The God And Father"
Tune: *Praise, My Soul,* 87 87 87
["Praise, My Soul, The King Of Heaven"]

1. Blesséd be our God and Father,
    God of Jesus Christ our Lord!
    By God's grace and steadfast mercy
    we were reborn through the Word
        to a living hope through Jesus'
        resurrection from the dead.

2. Our new birthright's held in heaven,
    fading not and ever pure,
    guarded by God's pow'r that keeps us,
    for, by faith, salvation's sure:

we do not possess it fully;
when the End comes, it's revealed.

3. With our eyes we've never seen Him,
yet we love Him, who loved us;
and Him trusting, we're rejoicing,
joy so full and glorious!
Faith in Christ has giv'n the outcome:
the salvation of our souls.

Pastoral Greeting

P: May grace and peace be abundantly yours.

C: **And yours as well.**

Pastoral Assurance

P: Remember:
You were not ransomed with money or precious metals,
but with the precious blood of Christ,
who is comparable to a faultless and unblemished
lamb;
who was foreknown before the foundation of the
universe,
but who was revealed in these, the Last of Times.
Through Christ you trust in God,
who raised Christ from the dead and gave him glory,
so that your faith and hope are anchored in God.

C: **Amen.**

Prayer of the Day

SIT

WORD

Scripture Readings

[Music is appropriate before or after any of the readings]

First Lesson

Psalm *[preferably sung]*

Second Lesson

STAND

Gospel Lesson

SIT

Sermon

STAND

Hymn of the Day

"Christ, Long By God Foreknown"
Tune: *Southwell,* SM
["Lord Jesus, Think On Me"]

1. Christ, long by God foreknown,
    has come in these Last Days
    to seek and save his wand'ring strays,
    to bring them back, his own.

2. Christ never sinned, nor lied,
    but trusted the just Judge;
    and when insulted, swore no grudge;
    while suff'ring, soft replied.

3. Our Lord Christ our sin bore
        up to the crúél cross;
            his tree-bound body ransomed loss;
    his wounds our peace implore.

4. Like sheep, we went astray,
        but now we are restored
            to our Good Shepherd, who outpoured
    his life; who guides our way.

Confession of Faith

APOSTLES' CREED

I believe in God, the Father almighty,
    creator of heaven and earth.

I believe in Jesus Christ, his only Son, our Lord.
    He was conceived in the power of the Holy Spirit
        and born of the virgin Mary.
    He suffered under Pontius Pilate,
        was crucified, died and was buried.
    He descended into hell.*
    On the third day he rose again.
    He ascended into heaven,
        and is seated at the right hand of the Father.
    He will come again to judge the living and the dead.

I believe in the Holy Spirit, the holy catholic Church,
    the communion of saints,
    the forgiveness of sins,
    the resurrection of the body,
    and the life everlasting. Amen.

*Or, *He descended to the dead.*

SIT

Offering

[An anthem, solo, or other music is appropriate here]

STAND

Offertory Canticle

"We Are A Chosen Race"
Tune: *Heath,* SM
["We Give Thee But Thine Own"]

1. We are a chosen race,
        a priestly, royal Kíngdóm,
    a holy nation, set apart
        to be God's very own.

2. That we may then declare
        God's wondrous deeds for us;
    God call'd us out of Darkness
        into God's Light marvelous.

Prayers and the Sharing of the Peace

[The ministers then prepare the bread and wine for the distribution. If Communion is not celebrated, the service continues with the **Hymn of the Cross,** *below]*

MEAL

Great Thanksgiving

P: The Lord be with you.

C: **And also with you.**

P: Lift up your hearts.

C: **We lift them up to the Lord.**

P: Let us thank the Lord our God.

C: **It is right to give God thanks and praise.**

Preface

P: It is Christ who was taken from the flock,
    and led to sacrifice.
At evening Christ was sacrificed,
    and in the Night he was buried.
Not one of his bones was broken on the Tree,
    and in the earth he suffered no decay.
Christ rose from the dead;
    he rose from the depths of the grave.
Like a sheep he was led away;
    like a lamb he was sacrificed.

C: Christ is the Lamb of God
    who removes the sin of the world.

P: It is Christ who covered Death with shame
    and threw the Powers into mourning,
        as Moses did Pharaoh.
It is Christ who struck down Iniquity
    and deprived Injustice of its children,
        as Moses did Egypt.
It is Christ who led us out
    from slavery to freedom,
    from Darkness to Light,
    from Death to Life,
    from tyranny to eternal liberation;
for Christ makes of us a new priesthood,
    and chosen people forever.

C: Amen.

Words of Institution

P: In the night in which he was betrayed,
    our Lord Jesus took bread and gave thanks;
    broke it, and gave it to his diciples, saying,
    "Take and eat; this is my body, given for you.

    Do this for the remembrance of me."

Again, after supper,
he took the cup, gave thanks
and gave it for all to drink, saying,
"This cup is the new covenant in my blood,
shed for you and for all people
for the forgiveness of sins.

Do this for remembrance of me."

Lord's Prayer

Our Father in heaven,
hallowed be your name,
your kingdom come,
your will be done,
on earth as in heaven.
Give us today our daily bread.
Forgive us our sins
as we forgive those
who sin against us.
Save us from the time of trial
and deliver us from evil.
For the kingdom, the power,
and the glory are yours
now and forever. Amen.

SIT

Distribution

[Congregational hymns, instrumental or vocal music may be used during the distribution]

STAND

Hymn of the Cross

"Life's Lord Is Crucified"
Tune: *St. Thomas,* SM
["I Love Thy Kingdom, Lord"]

1. Life's Lord is crucified
    and lifted up in shame;
    yet, lifted up, he's glorified;
    and draws us to his Name.

2. High on the tree he hangs,
    who hung the world in space;
    Life's Lord Death kills with Sin-soaked fangs;
    Life chokes in Dust's last place!

3. The Judge is judged unjust;
    the One who freed is bound!
    The hands that shaped all life from dust
    are pierc'd with wounds profound.

4, As by a tree came Death,
    so by a tree comes Life!
    Death, breathing murder with each breath,
    Life kills in love-filled strife.

5. The cross will death dispel,
    will break sin's crushing vise,
    will burst the gates of harrow'd hell,
    and open Paradise!

Pastoral Blessing

P: May the Body and Blood of our Lord Jesus Christ
    strengthen you and keep you in his grace.

C: Amen.

Pastoral Exhortation

P: The end of all things is at hand:
Therefore, be serious and discipline yourselves
for the sake of your prayers.
Above all, maintain constant love for one another,
for love covers a multitude of sins.

Hymn Response

"Beneath The Guarding Hand Of God"
Tune: *Dundee,* CM
["My God, How Wonderful Thou Art"]

1. Beneath the guarding hand of God
then let us humbly wait,
for in the right, the best of times,
God will us elevate.

2. Roll all your worries onto God,
whose strength will see you through.
Your God your stress and sorrow shares;
your God still cares for you.

SENDING

Benediction

P: Now may the God of all grace —
who called you to eternal glory in Christ —
restore, support, strengthen, and establish you.
To God be the glory and power forever and ever.

C: Amen.

Hymn

"Christ, Arisen, Stands And Cries"
Tune: *Salzburg,* 77 77 D
["Let The Whole Creation Cry"]

1. Christ, arisen, stands and cries,
   "Who with me will dare dispute?
   Come, present your argument;
   state your case, and mine refute!
   While on earth, I freed from sin,
   and did often death commute;
   won Life's vict'ry through defeat;
   to the death was resolute!

2. "I destroyed that monster, Death;
   triumphed o'er your Enemy!
   Under foot I tread down Hell;
   chained the Strong Man, took his key!
   Then I plundered all his house —
   you, his slaves, I swift set free!
   You I raised to Heaven's heights!
   Who will dare, then, gainsay me?

3. "Come, you sons of Adam's race,
   suff'ring still from Adam's Fall;
   come, Eve's daughters, gone from grace,
   come, be freed from Sin's fierce thrall:
   My forgiveness, come, receive;
   hear and heed my gracious call!
   No one else can set you free
   from Sin's grip and choking gall.

4. "I, the God-sent Paschal Lamb —
   I my blood have freely shed!
   I, your holiness and Life!
   I, your Rising from the dead!
   I, your Lord, will give you Light!
   I, your King — be not misled!
   I, once dead, arose again!
   I am your exalted Head!"

Sources for
"A Living Hope"
The Liturgical Witness Of First Peter

Entrance Hymn: 1 Peter 1:3-8
Pastoral Greeting: 1 Timothy 1:2
Hymn of the Day: 1 Peter 1:20; 2:21-24
Apostles' Creed: International Consultation on English Texts
Offertory Canticle: 1 Peter 2:9
Preface: Melito of Sardis, *On the Pascha,* 66-68
Lord's Prayer: International Consultation on English Texts
Hymn of the Cross: Melito of Sardis, *New Fragments II and III*
Pastoral Exhortation: 1 Peter 4:7-8
Hymn Response: 1 Peter 5:6-7
Benediction: 1 Peter 5:10-11
Hymn: Melito of Sardis, *On the Pascha,* 101-103

Unless otherwise noted, all translations, paraphrases, and versifications from
the Greek New Testament and that of Melito of Sardis are by Charles
M. Mountain.

12

The Liturgical Witness Of First John
[Easter 2-7, B]

"God Is Love"

GATHERING

[Prelude]

STAND

Entrance Canticle

"The Word Of Life"
Tune: *Bunessan,* 55 54 D
["Morning Has Broken"]

1. That which was from the
        very Beginning,
    what we have heard, and
        our eyes have seen;
    what we beheld, and
        our hands have handled,
    to you proclaim we:
        the Word of Life.

2. Life was revealed, and
   we have beheld it,
   and witness bear and
   to you proclaim
   Eternal Life, who
   was with the Father,
   who in the flesh was
   to us revealed.

3. What we have seen and
   heard, we share with you,
   so that you with us
   might fellowship;
   our fellowship is
   joy in the Father,
   made full in God's Son,
   in Jesus Christ.

Pastoral Greeting

L: Peace be with you.

C: **And also with you.**

Confession and Absolution

L: This is the announcement we heard from him and proclaim to you, that God is Light and in God there is no Darkness at all. If we say that we have fellowship with God, but walk in the Darkness, we lie and are not doing the truth; but if we walk in the Light just as God is in the Light, we have fellowship with one another, and the blood of Jesus, God's Son, cleanses us from all sin. If we say that we have no sin, we deceive ourselves, and the truth is not in us. If we confess our sins, God will forgive us our sins and cleanse us from all unrighteousness — for Christ is Faithful and Righteous.

C: Father, we confess that we do not love you fully, for we fail to love our Christian brother or sister fully. Forgive us our sin, and give us your Holy Spirit that we might have the power to live as Jesus lived, and to love as Jesus loved. Amen.

L: If anyone sins, we have an Advocate with the Father, Jesus Christ, the Righteous. And he is the atoning sacrifice for our sins; and not for our sins only, but also for the whole world. Hear, then, the Good News: Your sins are forgiven for Jesus' sake.

C: Amen.

Confessional Hymn

"This Will Our Hearts Assure"
Tune: *Leominster,* SMD
["Wide Open Are Your Hands"]

1. This will our hearts assure
       when they within condemn,
   that God is greater than our hearts —
       for God knows everything.
   Belovéd, if our hearts
       no longer us condemn,
   then we before God boldness have,
       and may ask anything!

2. And this is what we ask:
       that we keep God's commands;
   and this is first among them all,
       that we in Christ believe.
   The second follows close,
       the second great command,
   that from the heart each other love,
       and thus to God we cleave.

or

149

"Our God Is Love"
Tune: *Third Mode Melody,* CMD

1. Our God is love, and those who live
   in love, in God abide.
   And God abides and lives in them;
   they nothing need to hide.
   For love complete by this is known:
   that we with boldness stand
   on that great final Judgment Day
   'fore Christ at God's right hand.

2. For those who make the boastful claim
   of loving God unseen,
   but will not love their siblings near,
   God's son or daughter seen,
   are living still in Darkness' realm,
   and they themselves deceive;
   and on that final Judgment Day,
   will have just cause to grieve.

Prayer of the Day

SIT

WORD

Scripture Readings

[Music is appropriate before or after any of the readings]

[Said before the First Lesson]

This is God's commandment:
We should believe in the name
of God's Son, Jesus Christ;
and that we should love one another,
just as Christ commanded us.

First Lesson

Psalm *[preferably sung]*

Second Lesson

STAND

[Read before Gospel Lesson]

> This is what God promised us:
>> Eternal Life.

Gospel Lesson

SIT

Sermon

<u>Sermon Hymn</u>

"Beloved, Let Us Love One Another"
Tune: *Bunessan,* 55 54 D
["Morning Has Broken"]

1. Belovéd, let us
       love one another,
     for those who love are
       born from above,
     and they have known God;
       but they who love not,
     never have known God,
       for God is love.

2. This is the way God's
       pure love among us
     made its appearing
       to us, enslaved:
     God sent his Son, the
       only-Begotten,
     into the world; through
       him we are saved.

3. In this is love: Not
        that we have God loved,
    but God in love
        sent Christ from above.
    Christ is for sins the
        place of atonement.
    If God so loved us,
        so we should love.

STAND

Confession of Faith

THE CREED OF JOHN'S CIRCLE OF FRIENDS

God is love.
  God gave us Eternal Life.
This Life is in God's Son.
  God's Son is the atoning sacrifice for our sins.
Whoever has the Son, has Life;
  whoever has not the Son, does not have Life.

We love God because God first loved us.
Those who do not love a brother or sister
  whom they can see,
    cannot love God whom they have never seen.
The commandment we have from the Son is this:
  those who love God
    ought to love their brother and sister also.
By this we know that Christ abides in us, and we in him:
  by the Spirit which was given us. Amen.

or

APOSTLES' CREED

I believe in God, the Father almighty,
  creator of heaven and earth.

I believe in Jesus Christ, his only Son, our Lord.
  He was conceived in the power of the Holy Spirit
    and born of the virgin Mary.
  He suffered under Pontius Pilate,
    was crucified, died and was buried.
  He descended into hell.*
  On the third day he rose again.
  He ascended into heaven,
    and is seated at the right hand of the Father.
  He will come again to judge the living and the dead.

I believe in the Holy Spirit, the holy catholic Church,
  the communion of saints,
  the forgiveness of sins,
  the resurrection of the body,
  and the life everlasting. Amen

*Or, *He descended to the dead.*

Sharing of the Peace

SIT

Offering
[An anthem, solo, or other music is appropriate here]

STAND

Offertory Hymn

"Children Of God"
Tune: *Schönster Jesus,* 558 558
["Fairest Lord Jesus"]

1.   Look at the great love
        our Father's giv'n us:
            we're children of God, adopted, free!
      Belovéd, e'en now
        are we God's children;
            but still únknówn is what we'll be.

153

2. Of this we're sure: when,
       at last, we see him,
          as Christ is, we are sure to be.
    For we shall see him
       just as he is then.
          As Christ is púre, let's pure, too, be.

Prayers

Lord's Prayer

Our Father in heaven,
   hallowed be your name,
   your kingdom come,
   your will be done,
   on earth as in heaven.
Give us today our daily bread.
Forgive us our sins
   as we forgive those
   who sin against us.
Save us from the time of trial
   and deliver us from evil.
For the kingdom, the power,
   and the glory are yours
   now and forever. Amen.

SENDING

Blessing

L: We know that the Son of God has come,
       and has given us the necessary understanding
          to recognize what is true;
    and we are in the truth,
       in Jesus Christ, God's Son.
    This is the true God and Life Eternal.

C: **Amen.**

Hymn

"Since We Believe In Christ"
Tune: *Was frag Ich nach der Welt,* 67 67 66 66
["O God, My Faithful God"]

1. Since we believe in Christ,
        God's own Messiah, Jesus,
    we're truly born of God;
        and God from sin still frees us.
    For when we love the child,
        we love the parent too;
    for when we love, we keep
        all God's commandments too.

2. And since we're born of God,
        through Christ the world we've conquer'd;
    faith is the victory,
        for in God's Son we're anchor'd.
    Christ is the one who came
        by water and the blood.
    To Christ both testify,
        and hearts with Christ's love flood.

Sources for
"God Is Love"
The Liturgical Witness Of First John

Entrance Canticle: 1 John 1:1-4
Pastoral Greeting: 3 John 15
Confession and Absolution: 1 John 1:5-9; 2:1-2
Confessional Hymn: 1 John 3:19-24; 4:12 **or** 1 John 4:16-19
Reading before the First Lesson: 1 John 3:23
Reading before the Gospel Lesson: 1 John 5:11
Sermon Hymn: 1 John 4:4-7
Confession of Faith: Composite from 1 John
Offertory Hymn: 1 John 3:1-3
Lord's Prayer: International Consultation on English Texts
Blessing: 1 John 5:2-21
Hymn: 1 John 5:1-5

Unless otherwise noted, all translations, paraphrases, and versifications from the Greek New Testament are by Charles M. Mountain.

13

The Liturgical Witness Of Revelation
[New Year, ABC; Easter 2-7, C]

"Worthy The Lamb!"

Service of Holy Communion

GATHERING

[Prelude]

STAND

Entrance Hymn

"A Crowd, A Countless Multitude"
Tune: *Deo gracias,* LM
["Oh, Wondrous Type, O Vision Fair"]

1. A crowd, a countless multitude
       from ev'ry nation, tribe, and tongue
    before God's throne with palm leaves stood,
       and each to God with whole heart sung:

2. "Salvation," they with full voice tone,
       "to God Almighty e'er belongs,
    to God who sits upon the throne,
       and to the Lamb!" all heaven songs.

3. The white-robed throng before God's throne
   (in worship standing day and night) —
   God spreads o'er them a fail-safe zone;
   and none will harm or cause them fright.

4. Their Shepherd-Guide will 'fore them go,
   and lead to welling springs of Life.
   God wipes away their tears and woe;
   they safe remain from sin and strife.

Dialogue

A: To the one who loved us,
C: **and set us free from our sins by his blood,**
and made us kings,
and priests to his God and Father —
to Christ be the glory and power forever and ever.
Amen.

Behold, Christ is coming with the clouds,
and every eye will see him,
even those who pierced him,
and all the tribes of the earth will mourn.
Even so,
let it be!

Do not fear! I am the First
and I'm the Last — the Living One;
I once was dead —
but, look! I live forever and ever!
And I have the key to Death,
and I have unlocked Hell.

Hymn *[sung by all]*

Tune: *Praise, My Soul,* 87 87 87
["Praise, My Soul, The King Of Heaven"]

> **"I, the Alpha and Omega,**
> **I, the Future and the Past;**

The Beginning, and the Ending;
   Soon I come again — at last!"
Amen, amen! Come, Lord Jesus!
   Come, O bright and morning star!

Greeting

P: Grace and peace to you
      from the One who is, who was, and is to come,
  and from Jesus Christ, the Faithful Witness,
      the First-born from the dead,
         and the Ruler of earthly kings.

C: **Amen.**

Hymn of Praise

"Worthy!"
Tune: *Truro,* LM
["Christ Is Alive! Let Christians Sing"]

1.   Worthy are you, our Lord and God,
      the glory, honor to receive!
  To you the power e'er belongs;
      O God, our praise to you receive!

2.   Worthy are you, O Lamb of God,
      to take the Word — you are its key!
  For you were killed; and with your blood
      your captive people ransomed free!

3.   God's priestly Kingdom has been made
      from folk of ev'ry race and tongue;
  they reign, God's viceroys, o'er the earth,
      for they with whole hearts to God clung.

4.   Now to the One upon the throne,
      and Lamb who died, but lives again,
  blessing and honor, glory, might,
      now and forever be! Amen!

The Prayer of the Day

SIT

WORD

Scripture Readings

First Lesson

Psalm

Second Lesson

STAND

Gospel Lesson

SIT

Hymn of the Day
[The Hymn of the Day may also follow the Sermon]

Sermon

Confession of Faith
[The Nicene Creed may be said on Festival Days]

APOSTLES' CREED

**I believe in God, the Father almighty,
creator of heaven and earth.**

**I believe in Jesus Christ, his only Son, our Lord,
He was conceived by the power of the Holy Spirit
and born of the virgin Mary.
He suffered under Pontius Pilate,
was crucified, died, and was buried.**

He descended into hell.*
On the third day he rose again.
He ascended into heaven,
   and is seated at the right hand of the Father.
He will come again to judge the living and the dead.

I believe in the Holy Spirit, the holy catholic Church,
   the communion of saints,
   the forgiveness of sins,
   the resurrection of the body,
   and the life everlasting. Amen.

*Or, *He descended to the dead.*

Prayers and the Sharing of the Peace

Offering

[An anthem, solo, or other music is appropriate here]

STAND

Offertory Hymn

"How Great and Marvelous"
Tune: *Lobt gott, Ihr Christen,* 86 866
["Let All Creation Praise Its Lord"]

1.   How great and marv'lous are your works,
     our Lord, Almighty God!
   How true and righteous are your ways;
     all peoples give you laud,
     all peoples give you laud!

2.   O Lord, we hold your Name in awe;
     we glorify your name!
   For you are holy; and you are
     forevermore the same;
     forevermore the same!

Offertory Prayer

A: Lord God Almighty,

C: **we return only in part what you have first given us. To**

you belongs the world and all it contains, all the wealth, all the resources. Accept our gifts for Jesus' sake, your best gift of all. Amen.

[The ministers then prepare the bread and wine for distribution]

MEAL

Great Thanksgiving

P: The Lord be with you.

C: **And also with you.**

P: Lift up your hearts.

C: **We lift them up to the Lord.**

P: Let us thank the Lord our God.

C: **It is right to thank and praise God.**

Preface

P: Almighty and Everliving God; it is only right and fitting that we should praise you at all times and in every place:

For you sent to us the Lion of the tribe of Judah,
   who died as the Lamb of God on our behalf,
      that we might live.
We thank you for the salvation
   Christ provided for us.

And now we await our Lord Jesus' return
   in glory and honor and power
      as the King of kings, and Lord of lords.
"Behold, he is coming with the clouds;
   and every eye will see him.
      Amen."

Help us now to join the heavenly hosts
   which never cease to praise you,
      day or night:

or

[All sing]:

Tune: *Hymn to Joy,* 87 87 D
["Joyful, Joyful, We Adore Thee"]

> **Alleluia! for the Lord our**
> **God Almighty reigns on earth!**
> **All rejoice, exult, and glory,**
> **giving God due praise and worth!**
> **For the Marriage Feast has come;**
> **let us haste to celebrate.**
> **Bless'd those joined to Christ, their Bridegroom;**
> **nothing can them separate.**

P: Help us then, Almighty God,
> to join the heavenly hosts
> > which never cease to praise you,
> > > singing day and night:

Sanctus

"Holy, Holy, Holy"
Tune: *Nicaea,* 11 12 12 10
["Holy, Holy, Holy, Lord God Almighty"]

> **Holy, holy, holy, Lord God Almighty:**
> **who was, who is now, e'er the God who comes, the**
> **same!**
> **Holy, holy, holy, Lord of heaven's army;**
> **God's radiant glory heav'n and earth proclaim!**

Words of Institution

P: In the night in which he was betrayed,
> our Lord Jesus took bread and gave thanks;
> broke it, and gave it to his disciples, saying,
> "Take and eat; this is my body, given for you.
>
> Do this for the remembrance of me."

163

Again, after supper,
he took the cup, gave thanks
and gave it for all to drink, saying,
"This cup is the new covenant in my blood,
shed for you and for all people
for the forgiveness of sins.

Do this for remembrance of me."

Lord's Prayer

> **Our Father in heaven,**
> > **hallowed be your name,**
> > **your kingdom come,**
> > **your will be done,**
> > **on earth as in heaven.**
>
> **Give us today our daily bread.**
> **Forgive us our sins**
> > **as we forgive those**
> > **who sin against us.**
>
> **Save us from the time of trial**
> > **and deliver us from evil.**
>
> **For the kingdom, the power,**
> > **and the glory are yours**
> > **now and forever. Amen.**

SIT

Distribution

[Congregational hymns, instrumental or vocal music may be used during the distribution]

STAND

P: The Body and Blood of our Lord Jesus Christ
strengthen you and keep you in his grace.
For "they overcame by the blood of the Lamb,
and the word of their witness."

C: Amen.

Post-Communion Hymn

"We Give You Thanks"
Tune: *Lobt Gott, Ihr Christen,* 86 866
["Let All Creation Praise Its Lord"]

> We give you thanks, Almighty God,
> who was and is to come,
> that you have seized your sov'reign pow'r:
> to you must death succumb,
> to you death must succumb!

Maran-atha

A: With the Spirit and as the Bride, we cry out,
C: **"Our Lord, come!"**
With all creation, we cry out,
"Our Lord, come!"
With all those written down in the Lamb's Book of Life,
we cry out,
"Our Lord, Come!"
With St. John, and with the whole Church
on earth and in heaven, living and dead, we cry out:
"Amen. Come, Lord Jesus!"
Jesus testifies, "I am coming soon."
Even so, amen.
Come, O root and shoot of David;
Come, O bright and morning star!

SENDING

Benediction

P: The grace of the Lord Jesus be with you all.

C: Amen.

Canticle

"Consummation"
Tune: *Walton,* LM
["Jesus, Thou Joy Of Loving Hearts"]

1. God's home is now with humankind;
    God dwells with them; God's peóplé they are.
   God wipes away their ev'ry tear;
    and death itself shall live no more!

2. There shall be no more grief or pain;
    these former things have pass'd away.
   The Lamb and God are in their midst;
    there nothing more shall die accurs'd.

3. Their servants there shall worship them;
    God's face will they forever see!
   God's name they bear upon their brows;
    and God's are they forevermore.

4. And night there never overcomes;
    they need no light of lamp or sun.
   The Lord their God shall be their light;
    they reign, and that forevermore!

Sources for
"Worthy The Lamb!"
The Liturgical Witness Of Revelation

Entrance Hymn: Revelation 7:9-17
Dialogue and Hymn: Revelation 1:6-8
Greeting: Revelation 1:4-5
Hymn of Praise: Revelation 4:11; 5:9-10, 12-13
Apostles' Creed: International Consultation on English Texts
Offertory: Revelation 15:3-4
Preface: Revelation 5:5 **or** 19:6-9
Sanctus: Revelation 4:8 + Isaiah 6:3
Post-Communion Blessing: Revelation 12:11
Post-Communion Hymn: Revelation 19:15
Maran-atha: Revelation 22:17, 20
Benediction: Revelation 22:21
Canticle: Revelation 21:2-4; 22:3-5

Unless otherwise noted, all translations, paraphrases, and versifications from the Greek New Testament are by Charles M. Mountain.

14

The Liturgical Witness
Of The Early Church

[Mary, Mother of the Lord (August 15);
All Saints' (November 1); St. Stephen, Deacon
and Martyr (December 26); Sundays after
Christmas; Season of the Epiphany, including
The Baptism of the Lord; Days for the
Commemoration of people who lived in the first
centuries of the church (for example, Ignatius,
Polycarp, Irenaeus, and many more)]

"In Death, True Life"

Service of Holy Communion

GATHERING

[Prelude]

STAND

Entrance Hymn

"Astrological Disturbance"
Tune: *Morning Star,* 11 10 11 10
["Brightest And Best Of The Stars Of The Morning"]

1.   Look! That bright star, all the night's lights outshining!
     Radiant it gleams, though it beams from afar!

All other lights — e'en the lesser and great light —
all dance in worship 'fore that dazzling star.

2.	Light so superlative, star so disturbing —
n'er has its like in the Zodiac wheeled.
Thus from our trust in the stars this star frees us;
for Fortune's fate by this star's light was sealed.

3.	Breaks in God's Kingdom; Day shines in the Darkness;
God is a human, revealed to our sight;
newness of Life manifest in the Christ-Child:
led by this star, Magi came to the Light.

4.	From this time forth, nothing is as it has been —
our God has turned this world's way on its head!
Now Death will die, for the old kingdom passes:
"Come to us, Daystar; your Light on us shed!"

Pastoral Greeting

P:	May mercy and peace
be multiplied to you,
from God Almighty
and Jesus Christ, our Savior.

**C:	And also to you.**

Hymn of Praise

"Te Deum Laudamus"
Tune: *Hanover,* 10 10 11 11
["O Worship The King"]

1.	We praise you, O God, our Father and Lord;
the earth worships you, One God, with accord.
To you angels cry out, each heavenly pow'r,
with Cherubim, Seraphim, hour by hour:

2.	"Lord God — holy, holy, holy — of hosts;
both heaven and earth your great glory boasts!"
Th'Apostles still worship; the Prophets still praise;
the Martyrs an army to muster still raise.

3. And your holy Church, throughout all the earth,
      still raises its praise, proclaiming your worth,
   O Father of Jesus, your Infinite Son,
      who with Holy Spirit, our Couns'lor, is One.

4. O Christ, you are King of Glory alone!
      Though God's timeless Son, your death sins atone.
   In flesh from the Virgin, you died on the cross
      to save us from danger and infinite loss.

5. When you overcame death's sharp, killing sting,
      the great gates of heav'n wide open did fling.
   To you sitting there at God's right hand above
      we sing, "God incarnate, O infinite Love!"

Dialogue

A: We pray, therefore: Help your servants,
C: **whom you redeemed with your precious blood;**
      make them to be numbered
         among all your saints in glory everlasting.
      O Lord, save your people,
         and bless your inheritance!
      Reign over us,
         and lift us up forever!
      Day by day we magnify you,
         and worship your Name forevermore. Amen.

SIT

WORD

Scripture Readings
[Music is appropriate before or after any of the readings]

    First Lesson

Psalm *[preferably sung]*

Second Lesson

Gradual

Tune: *Vom Himmel hoch,* LM
["From Heaven Above To Earth I Come"]

> Awake, O sleeper, from the dead,
>> and Christ, the Lord, will give you Light!
> The Sun of Resurrection-pow'r,
>> Christ's rays will give you Light and Life!

STAND

Gospel Lesson

SIT

Hymn of the Day

"The Universe Is Cruciform"
Tune: *Third Mode Melody,* CMD

1. The universe is cruciform,
       for Christ died on a Tree,
   and Christ's obedience unto death
       reversed life's entropy.
   Our woes arose in Adam's time,
       when he and Eve — still free —
   chose freely God to disobey,
       duped by the Enemy.

2. Then sin and death came rushing in
       to fill the God-void space,
   its height, its depth, its length and breadth,
       its ev'ry time and place.
   With iron fist these tyrants ruled
       o'er all the human race!
   Enslaved, ashamed, we hid from God,
       estranged from Life and grace.

3. But must sin's rule be absolute?
      Must death dog all our days?
   Must hopelessness and deep despair
      reign on while life decays?
   No! On the Cross, the ransom-price —
      Life's Lord — by death defrays,
   and now arisen from the dead,
      the death of death displays!

4. For Christ is God's almighty Word,
      pervading space and time,
   its height, its depth, its length and breadth —
      Creation's paradigm.
   In Christ all things have proper place;
      in all things, Christ is prime.
   For Christ is Head of heav'n and earth,
      the lowly and sublime.

5. The universe is cruciform;
      the Cross shall all unite.
   The Cross's depth imprints the earth,
      its height lights heaven bright;
   it lengthens long from East to West,
      its open arms invite
   those scattered wide to gather in
      from sin's domain and night.

Sermon

STAND

Confession of Faith

APOSTLES' CREED

**I believe in God, the Father almighty,
  creator of heaven and earth.**

173

I believe in Jesus Christ, his only Son, our Lord.
  He was conceived in the power of the Holy Spirit
    and born of the virgin Mary.
  He suffered under Pontius Pilate,
    was crucified, died and was buried.
  He descended into hell.*
  On the third day he rose again.
  He ascended into heaven,
    and is seated at the right hand of the Father.
  He will come again to judge the living and the dead.

I believe in the Holy Spirit, the holy catholic Church,
  the communion of saints,
  the forgiveness of sins,
  the resurrection of the body,
  and the life everlasting. Amen.

*Or, *He descended to the dead.*

SIT

Offering

[An anthem, solo, or other music is appropriate here]

STAND

Offertory Hymn

"Now Let Us All Remember"
Tune: *Aurelia,* 76 76 D
["The Church's One Foundation"]

1.   Now let us all remember
     from where, by whom, our call;
  and how our Lord Christ suffered,
     and swallowed death's sour gall.
  Then how can we repay him?
     What currency will do
  to pay the debt we owe him?
     He died for me, for you.

2. What debts we ever owe him;
    what grace he freely gave!
   "My child," as father names us;
    Christ sought us, lost, to save.
   What tribute may we offer
    to barter for such gifts?
   We've nothing; so as beggars,
    hold fast the hand that lifts.

Prayers and the Sharing of the Peace

[The ministers here prepare the bread and wine for distribution. If Communion is not celebrated, the service continues with the Post-Communion Hymn, below]

MEAL

Anamesis

"At This, The End Of Ages"
Tune: *Aurelia,* 76 76 D
["The Church's One Foundation"]

1. At this, the End of Ages,
    to win our liberty,
   God's Son belov'd, Christ Jesus,
    was sent to set us free.
   As sov'reign Love Incarnate,
    Christ ruled from Calv'ry's Tree;
   and now we live the Triumph,
    the Time of Jubilee.

2. To win a people holy,
    to work God's gracious will,
   God's Word became a human,
    God's word to faithful fill.

Christ's seat of pow'r and vict'ry?
  Mount Calv'ry's lowly hill!
Cross-hung in shame and suff'ring,
  Christ kills death's pow'r to kill.

3. For Christ, to death deliver'd
    (a death he freely chose),
  has death, by death, defeated;
    Christ broke death's grip and rose!
  Christ underfoot hell tramples;
    and sin's rule overthrows;
  Christ, showing forth Life's rising,
    will Life to all disclose.

4. That Maundy night's betrayal,
    Christ took the bread and blessed:
    "Take, eat; this is my body;
    remember this bequest."
  He then took up the chalice,
    and spoke to each, his guest,
  "This is my blood, shed for you;
    this will my death attest."

5. O Lord, help us remember
    your love, whose longing ends
  in reconciliation —
    your love estrangement rends.
  We all were called, one Body;
    one Hope our faith defends;
  One God and Father o'er us;
    one Love links us as friends.

Words of Institution

P: In the night in which he was betrayed,
  our Lord Jesus took bread and gave thanks;
  broke it, and gave it to his disciples, saying,
  "Take and eat; this is my body, given for you.

  Do this for the remembrance of me."

176

Again, after supper,
he took the cup, gave thanks
and gave it for all to drink, saying,
"This cup is the new covenant in my blood,
shed for you and for all people
for the forgiveness of sins.

Do this for remembrance of me."

P: *[Lifting the cup:]*
We thank you, our Father, for this cup,
   full of the wine from the sacred vine of David,
and now revealed to us
   as the blood of Jesus Christ,
      your Holy Child.

C: **To you be the glory forever!**

P: *[Lifting a portion of the broken bread:]*
We thank you, our Father,
   for the life and the knowledge
you revealed to us through Jesus Christ,
   your holy Child.

C: **To you be the glory forever!**

P: As the grains that make up our bread —
   once scattered over the hills and fields —
were gathered together
   and became one in this loaf,
so may your church be gathered, O Lord,
   from the farthest ends of the earth
      into one priestly and royal people.

C: **For yours is the glory and power,**
   through Jesus Christ, forever.

P: And so we give you thanks, holy Father,
   for your Name,

your holy Name, which you have allowed
   to take up residence within our hearts;
and we thank you
   for the knowledge,
   the faith,
   and the immortality
which you made known to us
   through Jesus Christ, your Child.

C: To you be the glory forever!

Lord's Prayer

Our Father in heaven,
   hallowed be your name,
   your kingdom come,
   your will be done,
   on earth as in heaven.
Give us today our daily bread.
Forgive us our sins
   as we forgive those
   who sin against us.
Save us from the time of trial
   and deliver us from evil.
For the kingdom, the power,
   and the glory are yours
   now and forever. Amen.

SIT

Distribution

[Congregational hymns, instrumental or vocal music may be sung]

Post-Communion Hymn

"There Is But One Great Physician"
Tune: *Praise, My Soul,* 87 87 87
["Praise, My Soul, The King Of Heaven"]

1. There is but one great Physician,
    healing body, healing soul;
   made from flesh, yet made from Spirit;
    made like us, to make us whole.
   He was born a human being,
    yet 'fore time, was "I AM," Lord!

2. He became a mortal being;
    he, as human, was revealed.
   He, in death, our true life gave us;
    he, by death, has our life healed.
   Praise the One who cannot suffer,
    yet was crucified, our Lord!

3. He was born the child of Mary,
    yet 'twas God's child Mary bore.
   Once he suffered; but now risen,
    he can suffer death no more.
   Once was mortal, now immortal,
    he is Jesus Christ, our Lord!

STAND

Pastoral Blessing

P: May the Body and Blood of our Lord Jesus Christ,
    given and shed for you for the forgiveness of sins,
    assure you that you have already passed over
    from Darkness to Light.

C: Amen.

Post-Communion Prayer

A: Remember your church, O Lord;
      Rescue it from all evil,
        and bring it to maturity in your love;
      gather it from the four winds in your Kingdom,
        a Kingdom prepared for it before the beginning of
        time.

C: **For yours, O Lord, is the power and the glory forever.
Amen.**

A: Our Lord, come; and this Age pass away!

C: **Amen. Come soon, Lord Jesus!**

Hosanna

Tune: *Gelobt sei Gott,* 888 with Alleluias
["Good Christian Friends, Rejoice And Sing!"]

ALL: Hosanna to king David's son!
      Bless'd is the one in God's name come!
      Highest hosannas now be sung!
      O maran-atha, O maran-atha — "O, our Lord, come!"

Exhortation

A: Remember, then, beloved of God,
      Christ is the way
        by which we have found salvation.
      Through him we fix our eyes on the heights of heaven;
        through him we gaze — as in a mirror —
          upon the pure and exalted face of God.

      Through him the eyes of our hearts
        have been opened;
      through him our foolish and sin-darkened minds
        have been given Light;
      through him the Almighty willed
        that we might taste the knowledge of immortality.

C: **Thanks be to God!**

Thanksgiving Hymn for the Light

"The Night, Like Fog, Entombed Us"
Tune: *Aurelia,* 76 76 D
["The Church's One Foundation"]

1. The Night, like fog, entombed us,
      and Darkness filled our eye.
   We see, for God has willed it;
      God dissipates the Lie!
   Christ saw us, racked and ruined,
      upon the rocks, storm-blown,
   then mercy manifested,
      and heart-felt love made known.

2. From Nothing, Christ has called us;
      from Blindness into Sight;
   from Nothing, our existence
      he willed to live in Light!
   Once hopeless, hapless, hating,
      we lived in living death,
   till Christ breathed on us Spirit,
      God's own Life-giving Breath.

SENDING

Benediction

P: The Lord bless you
      and protect you.
   The Lord's face shine on you
      and receive you with grace.
   The Lord look upon you with favor,
      and give you peace.

C: Amen.

Sources for
"In Death, True Life"
The Liturgical Witness Of The Early Church

Entrance Hymn: Letter of Ignatius to the Ephesians 19:2-3

Pastoral Greeting: Letter of Polycarp to the Philippians, salutation

Hymn of Praise and Dialogue: *"Te Deum"* *(Apostolic Constitutions,* c 380 CE)

Gradual: Ephesians 5:14 + Clement of Alexandria, *Protrepticus IX*

Sermon Hymn: Irenaeus, *Epideixis,* 34

Apostles' Creed: International Consultation on English Texts

Offertory Hymn: Second Letter of Clement to the Corinthians 1:2-8

Anamesis: Anamesis IV, *The Lutheran Book of Worship, Minister's Desk Edition*

Words of Institution: International Consultation on English Texts

Liturgy Following: *Didachê* IX: 1-4 + X:2

Lord's Prayer: International Consultation on English Texts.

Post-Communion Hymn: Letter of Ignatius to the Ephesians 7:2

Post-Communion Prayer: *Didachê* X:5-6

Exhortation: First Letter of Clement to the Corinthians 36:1-2

Thanksgiving Hymn Response: Second Letter of Clement to the Corinthians 1:2-8

Benediction: Numbers 6:24-26

Unless otherwise noted, all translations, paraphrases, and versifications from the Greek New Testament or the Greek texts of "the Fathers" are by Charles M. Mountain.

Index

Liturgies Listed According To Their Order In The Common Lectionary Series

Series A

Advent Season: "The Day Of The Lord": *Thessalonian Letters*

Christmas Season: "The Saying Is Sure": *Pastoral Letters*

New Year: "Worthy The Lamb!": *Revelation*

Name Of Jesus (January 1): "Always In The Lord Rejoice!": *Philippians*

Epiphany Season: "The Saying Is Sure": *Pastoral Letters*

Day of the Epiphany: "One God And Father Of Us All": *Ephesians*

Epiphany 4-8: "One Lord, One Body": *Corinthian Letters*

Presentation Of The Lord (February 2): "Prophet, Priest And King": *Hebrews*

Ash Wednesday: "One Lord, One Body"; *Corinthian Letters*

Ash Wednesday and Lent: Chorale Service of Holy Communion: *Romans and Galatians*

Annunciation Of The Lord (March 25): "Prophet, Priest, And King": *Hebrews*

Palm/Passion Sunday: "Always In The Lord Rejoice!": *Philippians*

Holy Week: "The Bread Of Life": *John*

Maundy Thursday: "One Lord, One Body": *Corinthian Letters*

Good Friday: "Prophet, Priest And King": *Hebrews*

Resurrection Of The Lord: "One Lord, One Body": *Corinthian Letters*

Easter 2-7: "A Living Hope": *1 Peter*

Day Of The Ascension: "One God And Father Of Us All": *Ephesians*

Pentecost Season: "A Living Hope": *1 Peter*

Propers 7-19: Chorale Service Of Holy Communion: *Romans and Galatians*

Propers 20-23: "Always In The Lord Rejoice!": *Philippians*

Propers 24-28: "The Day Of The Lord": *Thessalonian Letters*

Reformation Day (October 31): Chorale Service Of Holy Communion: *Romans and Galatians*

Commemorations: "In Death, True Life": *The Early Church*

Series B

Advent Season: "The Day Of The Lord": *Thessalonian Letters*

Christmas Season: "The Saying Is Sure": *Pastoral Letters*

New Year: "Worthy The Lamb!": *Revelation*

Name Of Jesus (January 1): "Always In The Lord Rejoice!": *Philippians*

Epiphany Season: "The Saying Is Sure": *Pastoral Letters*

Day Of The Epiphany: "One God And Father Of Us All": *Ephesians*

Epiphany 2-9: "One Lord, One Body": *Corinthian Letters*

Presentation Of The Lord (February 2): "Prophet, Priest, And King": *Hebrews*

Transfiguration: "One Lord, One Body": *Corinthian Letters*

Ash Wednesday: "One Lord, One Body"; *Corinthian Letters*

Ash Wednesday and Lent: Chorale Service of Holy Communion: *Romans and Galatians*

Annunciation Of The Lord (March 25): "Prophet, Priest, And King": *Hebrews*

Palm/Passion Sunday: "Always In The Lord Rejoice!": *Philippians*

Holy Week: "The Bread Of Life": *John*

Maundy Thursday: "One Lord, One Body": *Corinthian Letters*

Good Friday: "Prophet, Priest, And King": *Hebrews*

Resurrection of the Lord: "One Lord, One Body": *Corinthian Letters*

Easter 2-7: "God Is Love": *1 John*

Day Of The Ascension: "One God And Father Of Us All":
  Ephesians
Pentecost Season: "A Living Hope": *1 Peter*
Propers 4-9: "One Lord, One Body": *Corinthian Letters*
Propers 10-16: "One God And Father Of Us All": *Ephesians*
Propers 12-16: "The Bread Of Life": *John*
Propers 22-28: "Prophet, Priest, And King": *Hebrews*
Reformation Day (October 31): Chorale Service Of Holy Communion: *Romans and Galatians*
Commemorations: "In Death, True Life": *The Early Church*

Series C
Advent and Christmas Season: "Through The Desert Clear A Highway!": *Luke*
Advent Season: "The Day Of The Lord": *Thessalonian Letters*
Advent 2-3: "Always In The Lord Rejoice!": *Philippians*
Christmas Season: "The Saying Is Sure": *Pastoral Letters*
New Year: "Worthy The Lamb!": *Revelation*
Name Of Jesus (January 1): "Always In The Lord Rejoice!":
  Philippians
Epiphany Season: "The Saying Is Sure": *Pastoral Letters*
Day Of The Epiphany: "One God And Father Of Us All":
  Ephesians
Epiphany 2-9: "One Lord, One Body": *Corinthian Letters*
Presentation Of The Lord (February 2): "Prophet, Priest, And King": *Hebrews*
Transfiguration: "One Lord, One Body": *Corinthian Letters*
Ash Wednesday: "One Lord, One Body"; *Corinthian Letters*
Annunciation Of The Lord (March 25): "Prophet, Priest, And King": Hebrews
Palm/Passion Sunday: "Always In The Lord Rejoice!":
  Philippians
Holy Week: "The Bread Of Life": *John*
Maundy Thursday: "One Lord, One Body": *Corinthian Letters*
Good Friday: "Prophet, Priest, And King": *Hebrews*

Resurrection of the Lord: "One Lord, One Body": *Corinthian Letters*

Easter 2-7: "Worthy The Lamb!": *Revelation*

Day Of The Ascension: "One God And Father Of Us All": *Ephesians*

Pentecost Season: "A Living Hope": *1 Peter*

Propers 4-9: Chorale Service Of Holy Communion: *Romans and Galatians*

Propers 10-13: "Lordship And Unity": *Colossians*

Propers 14-17: "Prophet, Priest, And King": *Hebrews*

Propers 19-25: "The Saying Is Sure": *Pastoral Letters*

Propers 26-28: "The Day Of The Lord": *Thessalonian Letters*

Reformation Day (October 31): Chorale Service Of Holy Communion: *Romans and Galatians*

Commemorations: "In Death, True Life": *The Early Church*

Topical Bibliography

Basic Texts:
New Oxford Annotated Bible [New Revised Standard Version], edited by Bruce M. Metzer and Roland E. Murphy (Oxford University Press, New York, 1991).

Novum Testamentum Graece, edited by Kurt Aland, *et al* (Deutsche Bibelstiftung, Stuttgart, 1979, 26th edition).

The Revised Common Lectionary: The Consultation on Common Texts (Abingdon Press, Nashville, 1992).

Septuaginta, edited by Alfred Rahlf (Deutsche Bibelgesellschaft, Stuttgart, 1935).

Biblical Eschatology:
Gowan, Donald E., *Eschatology in the Old Testament* (Fortress Press, Philadelphia, 1986).

Ladd, George Eldon, *The Presence of the Future* (Wm. B. Eerdmans Publishing Co., Grand Rapids, 1974, 2nd edition).

Wainright, Geoffrey, *Eucharist and Eschatology* (Epworth Press, London, 1971).

New Testament Hymns: Form, Background and Content:
Aulén, Gustaf, *Christus Victor* (Macmillan Publishing Co., New York, 1969).

Breck, John, *The Shape of Biblical Language: Chiasmus in the Scriptures and Beyond* (St. Vladimir's Seminary Press, Crestwood, NY, 1994).

Deichgräber, Reinhard, *Gotteshymnus und Christushymnus in der frühen Christenheit* (Vandenhoech & Ruprecht, Göttingen, 1967).

Gloer, W. Hulitt, "Homologies and Hymns in the New Testament: Form, Content, and Criteria for Identification," in *Perspectives in Religious Studies,* Summer, 1984, Volume 11, No. 2 (Mercer University Press, Macon, 1984), pp. 115-132.

Hengel, Martin, "Hymn and Christology," in *Studia Biblica 1978: III. Papers on Paul and Other New Testament Authors* (Journal for the Study of the New Testament, Supplement Series, 3, Sheffield, 1980), pp. 173-197.

Kroff, Josef, *Die Christliche Hymnodik* (Wissenschaftliche Buchgeselschaft, Darmstadt, 1921-22, reprinted in 1968).

Martin, Ralph P., "Hymns in the New Testament: An Evolving Pattern of Worship Responses," in *Ex Auditu: An International Journal of Theological Interpretation of Scripture,* Vol. 8: "Worship" (Pickwick Publications, Allison Park, PA, 1992), pp. 33-44.

———— "Patterns of Worship in New Testament Churches," in *Journal for the Study of the New Testament,* 37 (JSNT Press, Sheffield, 1989), pp. 59-85.

———— *Reconciliation: A Study of Paul's Theology* (John Knox Press, Atlanta, 1981).

Mountain, Charles M., " 'Glory, Honor, and Blessing': The Hymns of the Apocalypse," in *The Hymn: A Journal of Congregational Song* (The Hymn Society in the United States and Canada, Ft. Worth, January, 1996).

———— "The New Testament Christ-Hymn," in *The Hymn: A Journal of Congregational Song,* January, 1993, pp. 20-28.

———— "The New Testament Epiphany-Hymn," in *The Hymn: A Journal of Congregational Song,* April, 1994, pp. 9-17.

———— *New Testament Scriptures for Singing* (Fairway Press, Lima, OH, 1990)

Sanders, Jack T., *New Testament Christological Hymns* (Cambridge University Press, Cambridge, 1971).

Schille, Gottfried, *Frühchristliche Hymnen* (Evangelische Verlagsanstalt, Berlin, 1965).

Wengst, Klaus, *Christologische Formeln und Lieder des Urchristentums* (Gütersloh Verlaghaus, Gütersloh, 1972).

Synoptic Gospels:
Brown, Raymond E., *The Birth of the Messiah* (Doubleday, New York, 1977).
Goulder, M.D., *The Evangelists' Calendar: A Lectionary Explanation of the Development of Scripture* (SPCK, London, 1972).
Iglesias, Salvador Muñoz, *Los evangelios de la infancia: I: Los cánticos del evangelio de la infancia según san Lucas* (Biblioteca de autores cristianos, Madrid, 1990, segunda edición).

Gospel According to John:
Correll, Alf, *Consummatum est* (The Macmillan Company, New York, 1958).
Cullman, Oscar, *Early Christian Worship* (SCM Press, London, 1953).
Durkin, Kenneth, "A Eucharistic Hymn in John 6?" in *Expository Times,* Vol. 98, March, 1987, pp. 168-170.
Raney, W.H., *The Relation of the Fourth Gospel to the Christian Cultus* (Alfred Töpelmann, Giessen, 1933).

Ephesians/Colossians:
Burger, Christoph, *Schöpfung und Versöhnung: Studien zum liturgischen Gut im Kolosser- und Epheserbrief* (Neukirchener Verlag, Tübingen, 1975).
Cannon, George E., *The Use of Traditional Materials in Colossians* (Mercer University Press, Macon, 1983).
Kirby, John C., *Ephesians, Baptism and Pentecost* (McGill University Press, Montreal, 1968).

Philippians:
Hofius, Otfried, *Der Christushymnus Philipper 2:6-11* (S.C.B. Mohr [Paul Siebeck], Tübingen, 1991, expanded edition).
Martin, Ralph P., *Carmen Christi* (Wm. B. Eerdmans Publishing Co., Grand Rapids, 1983, revised edition).
Robuck, Thomas Durward, *The Christ-Hymn in Philippians: A Rhetorical Analysis of Its Function in the Letter* (Unpublished dissertation, Southwest Baptist Seminary, Fort Worth, 1988).

The "Pastoral" Letters and Hebrews:

Horning, Estella, *Hymns in Hebrews: A Formal and Christological Analysis* (Unpublished dissertation, Northwestern University, Evanston, 1983).

Knight, George W., *The Faithful Sayings in the Pastoral Letters* (J.H. Kok, N.V. Kampden, Amsterdam [?], 1968).

1 Peter:

Boismard, Marie Emile, *Quatre hymns baptismale dans la premier épistre Pierre* (Les Edicions du Cerf, Paris, 1961).

Cross, F.L., *1. Peter: A Paschal Liturgy* (A.R. Mowbray and Co., London, 1954).

Perspectives on First Peter, edited by Charles H. Talbert (Mercer University Press, Macon, 1986).

1 John:

Malatesta, Edward, *Interiority and Covenant* (Biblical Institute Press, Rome, 1978).

Mountain, Charles, "Himnos en la primera carta de san Juan" (Unpublished paper written for a graduate class at St. Thomas Seminary, Denver, 1990).

Revelation:

Jörns, Klaus-Peter, *Das hymnische Evangelium* (Gütersloh Verlaghaus, Gütersloh, 1971).

Harris, Michael Anthony, *The Literary Function of Hymns in the Apocalypse of John* (Unpublished dissertation, The Southern Baptist Theological Seminary, 1989).

Mowry, L., "Revelation 4-5 and Early Christian Liturgical Usage," in *Journal of Biblical Literature,* (1952), pp. 75-84.

Shepherd, M.H., *The Paschal Liturgy and the Apocalypse* (Lutterworth, London, 1960).

Thompson, Marianne Meye, "Worship in the Book of Revelation," in *Ex Auditu: An International Journal of Theological Interpretation of Scripture,* Vol. 8: "Worship" (Pickwick Publications, Allison Park, PA, 1992), pp. 45-54.

Post-Apostolic Fathers (The Early Church):

"Carta de san Ignacio Mártir a los efesios," in *Padres apostólicos,* ed. by Daniel Ruiz Bueno (Biblioteca de autores cristianos, Madrid, 1967), pp. 447-459.

"Carta de san Ignacio Mártir a Policarpo," in *Padres apostólicos,* ed. by Daniel Ruiz Bueno (Biblioteca de autores cristianos, Madrid, 1967), pp. 496-502.

"Carta primera de san Clemente a los corintos," in *Padres apostólicos,* ed. by Daniel Ruiz Bueno (Biblioteca de autores cristianos, Madrid, 1967), pp. 177-238.

"Carta segunda de san Clemente a los corintos," in *Padres apostólicos,* ed. by Daniel Ruiz Bueno (Biblioteca de autores cristianos, Madrid, 1967), pp. 335-374.

Deiss, Lucien, *Springtime of the Liturgy* (Liturgical Press, Collegeville, 1979).

Melito of Sardis: "On Pascha" and "Fragments," ed. by Stuart George Hall (At the Clarendon Press, Oxford, 1979).

Niederwimmer, Kurt, *Die Didaché* (Vandenhoech & Ruprecht, Göttingen, 1989).

Richardson, Cyril C., translator and editor, *et al., Early Christian Fathers* (The Westminster Press, Philadelphia, 1953).

Appendix

Ten Sermons
For Use With These Liturgies

1

The Liturgical Witness Of Luke

"Mary — Luke's Model Christian"

It seems that through the centuries there were only two ways of talking about Mary: either to exalt her as a virtual substitute for Christ; or simply to ignore her. Luke, however, gives us a third alternative. He saw Mary as a model, a flesh and blood paradigm, of what God looks for in every one of us. For she is one of those few in Luke's Gospel who are living examples of Jesus' own words, "Bless'd ... are those who *hear the Word of God* and *keep it*" (Luke 11:28).

I.

A. Mary "heard the Word of God." When Luke uses this expression he means much more than a passive perception of sound waves. For Luke, to "hear" the Word of God also means to *believe and act* on that Word; to "hear" in this sense means to respond with complete confidence and total trust in the promise. And this is exactly what Mary did. She heard the words of God's messenger, believed them, and then acted on them: first with her song of praise; and then with her parenting of God's holy child. Her "faith-full" reply to Gabriel says it all, "Let it happen as you say." What an amazing woman! To hear, believe, and act on such crazy promises — God saw in her the "good and faithful heart" that God wants to create in all of us.

Nonetheless, God did not speak to her directly. God's Word came to Mary as it comes to us all: through means, through

195

instruments, through messengers. We receive the Word of God through one "angel" or another. Yes, even we are visited by angels, for the Greek word translated as "angel" [αγγελος] can also be rendered as "messenger." Now it's true that most of God's messengers do not appear so angelic — at least, outwardly. But they are just as useful as Gabriel was. Perhaps it was your pastor or your parents, or your Sunday School teacher; perhaps it was a hymn or anthem; or just some guy on the street — God used one or more of these "angels," these "messengers," to bring the great and precious promises home to your heart and life. The angels are there. They just don't always have wings.

Mary's response to the heavenly messenger was a simple one: "Let it be unto me according to your word." In other words, *carpe diem*. "Seize the day; let's go."

What a contrast to the response Gabriel received from Zechariah, the future father of John the Baptist! He too received great and precious promises about his son, a son that was to be born to him and his wife, Elizabeth, in their old age. Gabriel said to him:

> *"[John] will turn the people of Israel*
> *to the Lord their God.*
> *With the spirit and power of Elijah*
> *he will go before [the Lord],*
> *to turn the hearts of parents to their children,*
> *and the disobedient to the wisdom of the righteous,*
> *to make ready a people*
> *prepared for the Lord."*   (Luke 1:16-17, NRSV)

This is all a father could hope for in a son — or daughter, for that matter. But Zechariah's response was not Mary's. He said, "How will I know this will happen? Look, my wife and I are old. How can we have children now?" (Luke 1:18). (For some reason he did not recall the other miraculous births recorded in scripture, especially the birth of Samuel to Hannah.) The direct result of his unbelief was muteness. He would not be able to speak until John was born. Mary believed the Word and was enabled to praise; Zechariah did not receive the Word in faith, and was struck dumb. But God is good, and when John was born, Zechariah's tongue was loosed and he blessed God: "Bless we the Lord God," his newly loosened tongue proclaimed. "God has remembered the people and kept the promises."

Mary, though, did not have to wait. She heard the promise from the messenger, believed it, and acted on it. And what a strange, yea, bizarre, promise: no sex, but with child; not yet married, but a baby on the way. It must have been a tremendous burden for a teenage single mother in those days — even harder than now. Yet Mary was able to praise God and experience that "joy that passes understanding," the joy given by the Holy Spirit: "My soul magnifies the Lord, and my spirit rejoices in God my Savior," she sang. And why? "For the almighty God has done great things for me, and holy is God's name."

B. "Well, yes," you might respond, "but Mary, Zechariah, Elizabeth, and the others in the Bible were not like us. They were more spiritual and lived in a time when miracles were expected." To be sure, culturally they were in another world from ours. But in their humanity — their flesh and blood natures — they were just like us. The strange and puzzling announcements of supernatural intervention by God were not the sort of thing that happened to them every day. These were no "Super-Saints" who were somehow more acceptable to God than others. Nor were they "genetically religious," as some have brown eyes and others have blue; they were not born religious. Nor can we assume that Mary and the others had a backlog of merits, good works, or holy character that somehow made them God's favorites. Even the oft-repeated expression, "Hail, Mary, full of grace! The Lord is with you," does not mean that Mary had somehow been topped off with some "stuff" called "grace." Grace is not something you possess. "Full of grace" is a metaphor. "Grace" is God's love and choice of people who are unworthy and deserve nothing.

Grace is first and foremost a relationship, as the words, "The Lord is *with you*," plainly say. Mary, therefore, *was special because she was chosen; not chosen because she was special.*

Indeed, humanly speaking, Mary had little to commend her to God or anyone else. She was probably poor, uneducated, very young (probably 12 to 14 years old), and would, therefore, have no property and social status. And worst of all — at least from the point of view of the "upper crust" in Jerusalem — she hailed from that backwater of a border town, Nazareth. How could anything good come out of that polluted ghetto?

But God is not dependent on human standards. When Mary visited the other miraculous mother in this story, Elizabeth, we read that John leaped in Elizabeth's womb, and that Elizabeth herself was filled with the Holy Spirit and began to prophesy: "Blessed are you among women, and blessed is the fruit of your womb . . . . And blessed is she who believed that there would be a fulfillment of what was spoken to her by the Lord" (Luke 1:42, 45, NRSV).

Mary *heard the Word of God, believed it, and acted on it.*

II.

A. But there is much more for us to learn from Mary. She not only *heard* the Word of God, she *kept* it, even in the face of its apparently total failure. The crisis came when her firstborn son was betrayed, tortured, and executed on a cross. The disaster at Skull Hill seemed to mock every promise given to her about her son:

- "He will be great," yet here he is dying a criminal's death after a life of poverty and obscurity.
- "He will be called the Son of the Most High," yet was accused of being possessed by demons, a drunkard and a glutton, a friend of undesirables.
- "Of his Kingdom there will be no end," yet here he is, wrapped in a purple robe. The only ones who honor him — and that mockingly — are Herod's soldiers, the ones who

198

have just now beaten him, whipped him, and who will soon nail him up to die.

To the human mind these are not the trappings and signs of power that belong to any legitimate king and his kingdom. Yet Mary did not run away from Jesus as his disciples did. In John's account of the crucifixion we find her on the hill with her son, watching to the bitter end.

One of the older hymns of the church summarizes things well enough:

> At the Cross, her station keeping,
> Stood the mournful mother weeping,
>   Where he hung, the dying Lord,
> For her soul, of joy bereavéd,
> Bowed with anguish, deeply grievéd,
>   Felt the sharp and piercing sword.   *Cf. Luke 2:35*

> For his people's sins chastiséd,
> She beheld her Son despiséd,
>   Scourged, and crowned with thorns entwined;
> Saw him then from judgment taken,
> And in death by all forsaken,
>   Till his spirit he resigned.
> *(Eighth century, tr. Edward Caswall and others)*

But her glimpse of her son as he lay in death was not to be her last. For on the third day God raised up Jesus from the dead. And with his resurrection from the dead came the resurrection of all the promises God gave her. They took another form than what she may have supposed, but they were fulfilled nonetheless. Now Jesus was "great," and was declared "the Son of Most High," and was given a Kingdom that would "never end."

B. Mary is mentioned two more times in the New Testament. And both of these brief glimpses of her life after Christ's resurrection are very helpful for us who also want to follow him. The first of these places is found in Acts, chapter 1. Here we read how the disciples gathered together in Jerusalem after Jesus' ascension. The remaining eleven disciples are named. Then we read:

> *All these were constantly devoting themselves to prayer, together with certain women, including Mary, the mother of Jesus, as well as his brothers* (Acts 1:14, NRSV).

She was among those awaiting the outpouring of the Holy Spirit. Although she is not mentioned by name, I believe she was among those 120 upon whom the Spirit fell on the Day of Pentecost. For we read that "they were all together in one place" (Acts 2:1). She too was saved by grace alone and was granted the Holy Spirit, just like you and me.

The other place in scripture where Mary is mentioned is in John 2, the famous wedding at Canaan. I believe that her words on this occasion are the best ones to remember her and her role in salvation history. Here the privileged, "grace-full" vehicle for bringing the Savior into the world relates to us how we should regard her and her son. Her focus is entirely on Christ's person and works. And her witness is just as valid now as it was when she first spoke those words: **"Do everything he tells you to do"** (John 2:5). Then we too will be among those blest who "hear the word of God, and keep it." Amen.

2

The Liturgical Witness Of John

"I Am The Resurrection And The Life"

I was not looking for his name on the list of new admissions to the hospital. But there it was. I had originally planned to call on someone else (now recovered and sent home). I only discovered his name while checking for others in the parish I may have missed.

Jim. That is his name. What was he doing here? He and his wife lived in the northwestern corner of the state. Then I remembered that this hospital was the regional center for cancer patients. My heart quickened its pace even as my feet hurried to his room.

On the elevator to his floor my mind's eye saw Jim and his wife in their overly large, ranch-style home. (Jim's wife was mildly claustrophobic.) I could plainly see Jim's tall, thin form awkwardly folded into his chair like a jackknife. There he would sit with his pipe, calm and quiet. Jim was a carpenter, a maker of things. His house and many others bore all of the signs of caring, creative workmanship. I could also see his wife, only two-thirds his height, flitting about like the biblical Martha, anxious and worried about many things — in this case, a sumptuous supper of Swedish meatballs, mashed potatoes, and all the *lefse* and coffee you could hold. Their house had been a special place for my wife and me, a place as close to home as we had ever felt in our new location. The warmth of the place did not radiate from their hearth alone.

201

As I approached his hospital room, I could see him. He lay on his back, his thin build looking even thinner beneath the flimsy hospital gown. His wife sat opposite him talking with their daughter. Her gaze was focused on the small park and pond across the street, full of ducks and turtles, surrounded by a kaleidoscopic swirl of children and family pets, all enjoying the early Spring sun.

"Hi, Jim," I said on entering, reaching for his hand. "Well, hello, Chuck! Hey, Mom, look who's here," he said to his wife, crushing my hand in his strong, sure workman's grip. "Oh, Chuck," his wife said, "I'm so glad you're here. I've been praying a pastor would come by and here you are . . . ." Her voice trailed off into a choking sob.

Now I knew something was really wrong. Jim's daughter saw my face and answered my silent question. "Pastor, Dad has lung cancer. And it's terminal." I knew she did not mean to put it so bluntly; when your heart is full of pain your head does not always come up with the best choices.

We all sat down after that, trying to absorb what this all meant.

And Jim? What an amazing fellow! He was taking it better than any of us. "Well," he said, "it's all right. I've had a long and full life. I know that my Redeemer lives and will give me eternal life."

The death of Lazarus suddenly came to my mind. "John 11 made flesh and dwelling among us," I thought to myself. I could tell that these words were not said merely to soften his family's pain. They came from the heart, a heart full of faith and the Holy Spirit.

Soon after this, Jim's wife and daughter left briefly to get a snack. Jim and I talked awhile about his life and the times we were together in their home. Then our conversation lapsed into silence.

Finally, I asked, "Would it be all right if I read some scripture and we prayed together?" "Yes," was the quiet, strong response. I turned to John 11. Every word seemed to have been written with Jim and his family in mind. His daughter might have said with Martha, "Lord, if you had been here, my father would not have died." Without her saying it, I could sense that Jim's daughter felt that God had deserted them in their time of need. Jim's wife was in John 11, too. Like Mary, she had been sitting numb and desolated in her time of loss.

At that time, more than ever, we all needed to see Jesus at the gravesite of his friend, Lazarus. We needed to hear those two precious words from the scriptures, "Jesus wept." Yes, it is true that we worship Jesus as God and that in him all the fullness of Deity dwells. But we also worship and love him as our fellow human, one who knows our pains and sorrows, our joys and triumphs, firsthand. Jesus promised us, "I know my own and my own know me." And this Shepherd never loses track of the least of his flock.

And yes, Jim was in John 11, too. Jim's quiet acceptance of his whole situation fairly shouted his confidence in Jesus' words, "I am the Resurrection and the Life. The one believing in me, even though that one dies, yet shall that person live; and whoever lives and believes in me will never die."

As we prayed together, I knew that God had visited us all that glad-yet-sad Spring day. What else can we do when staring into the hollow eyes of Death except to seize the victory over Death by Jesus Christ, and to say, "Because Jesus lives, so shall I. I am united to his life, death, and resurrection by Baptism and faith. In Christ, *even I* shall live, though I die."

One Reformation hymn writer got it right:

> Jesus, my redeemer, lives;
> I, too, unto life shall waken.
> He will bring me where he is;
> Shall my courage, then, be shaken?
> Shall I fear, or could the head
> Rise and leave his members dead?
>
> No, too closely am I bound
> Unto him by hope forever;
> Faith's strong hand the rock has found,

Grasped it, and will leave it never;
Even death now cannot part
From it Lord the trusting heart. Amen[1]

---

1. Stanzas 2 and 3 of "Jesus Christ, My Sure Defense," by Louisa Henrietta, Electress of Brandenburg (1633) and translated by Catherine Winkworth.

3

The Liturgical Witness Of Romans And Galatians

"I Hope In God Alone"

"From Deepest Need"

1. From deepest need I cry to you,   *Psalm 130*
    O Lord God, hear and heed my cry!
    O turn a gracious ear to me,
    my urgent prayer do not deny.
       If you regard our sin and wrong,
       who could you rightly justify?

2. With you will only grace prevail
    that you our sense of sin erase!
    With you good works will not avail —
    sin will the best of lives deface!
       The bold and foolish, let them boast!
       but you we fear — and love your grace.

3. And so I hope in God alone,
    and not on my own virtues build.
    On God my heart will heedless lean —
    the God who's good, whose Word good willed.
       This is my comfort and my shield;
       my anxious heart by hope is stilled.

4. Though watching wakeful through the night,
   then watching weary through the day,
   my heart will still in God's will trust —
   no doubt or worry will me sway.
     Thus does true Israel, Spirit-born,
     who hopes in God — let come what may!

5. It's true that we are full of sin;
   yet God with grace is flowing o'er!   Romans 5:5, 15-17, 20-21
   God's helping hand no hindrance knows,
   though shame wells up within our core.
     Good Shepherd, gracious God, forgive
     your Israel's sins, her life restore!

Luther wrote this setting of Psalm 130 from the "deepest need" of two kinds: his own deep spiritual need for the assurance of the forgiveness of sins, and his deep need for new materials for Reformation worship.

"From Deepest Need" appears to have been written sometime near the end of 1523, for Luther wrote to his friend, Spalatin:

> *I intend, after the example of the prophets and the church*
> *Fathers, to create German psalms for the people, that is,*
> *spiritual hymns, that the Word of God might find a place*
> *among the people in song. We seek, above all else, poets.*
> *Since you are so skilled and proficient in German, I ask*
> *you to lend us a hand and to try to make a psalm into*
> *a hymn, as the example you have of mine. [Luther prob-*
> *ably refers here to his own psalm paraphrase, "From*
> *Deepest Need."] I want you, however, to avoid "flow-*
> *ery" language. The ideas addressed to the common peo-*
> *ple should be simple and easy to understand, yet pure*
> *and proper, corresponding as closely as possible to the*
> *original meaning of the psalm.*[1]

These are great principles for any aspiring hymn writer to follow! However, Spalatin never responded. But we still have the application of Luther's principles for writing "the [sung] Word made flesh" in his own German psalm, "From Deepest Need."

I

Stanza one reads:

> From deepest need I cry to you,
> O Lord God, hear and heed my cry!
> O turn a gracious ear to me,
> my urgent prayer do not deny.
>> If you regard our sin and wrong,
>> who could you rightly justify?

The first stanza of "From Deepest Need" proclaims the nature of the God with whom we have to do. This God is the God who hears and answers prayer, especially the prayer we pray in our hour of deepest need.

1. *"Out of the depths I cry to you."* As the scriptures bear witness, the people's cry is the beginning of God work. Their cry is the point of entry into whole saving and redeeming work that is spun out in history. For when the Israelites had become virtual slaves to the Egyptian Pharaohs, we read that

> *the Israelites groaned under their slavery, and cried out. Out of the slavery their cry for help rose up to God. God heard their groaning, and God remembered [the] covenant with Abraham, Isaac, and Jacob. God looked upon the Israelites, and God took notice of them* (Exodus 2:23-25, NRSV).

And in another place:

> *"I have observed the misery of my people ... I have heard their cry ... I know their sufferings, and I have come down to deliver them from the Egyptians, and to bring them out of that land"* (Exodus 3:7-8, NRSV).

Look at the verbs that the writer piles up to help us get the point: *heard, remembered, looked upon, took notice, observed,* and *know.* The last verb, "to know," is particularly strong. In the Hebrew it means a lot more than just recognizing facts. It means to know on a personal, intimate level, to actually participate in or experience firsthand. So when it says that God "knows" the sufferings of the people, it means that their suffering is God's, that their slavery is God's, that their cry enters into God's heart and is felt by God in the innermost recesses of God's being.

This is the God with whom we have to do, a God not aloof or indifferent to our needs and hurts, but a God who enters personally into our history and even participates in it. All through the Hebrew Bible we see God at work in a personal way in the Exodus and several centuries later in the return of the people from Exile. Over and over God hears the people's cry and answers their prayer. Isaiah writes: "In all their affliction [God] was afflicted ... in ... love and pity [God] redeemed them" (Isaiah 63:9, RSV).

2. This loving God wants us to pray this way to God that our slavery to sin be removed. In our hymn, Luther asks rhetorically, *"If you regard our sin and wrong, who could you rightly justify?"* Luther's original German reads, "If you regard our sin and wrong, who could before you stand?" Who, indeed, could stand before the Judge of all and plead "not guilty"? Who would not shrivel under the withering stare of the Ultimate Bar of the cosmos? Who could expect to receive the sentence of "justified"? I think you know the answer already.

II.

But Luther does not leave us dangling on the barbed wire of our sin. He provides the wire cutters that breach all barriers with these words:

> With you will only grace prevail
> that you our sense of sin erase!
> With you good works will not avail —
> sin will the best of lives deface!
> The bold and foolish, let them boast!
> But you we fear — and love your grace.

There is only one way that God may be approached by sinful human beings. We must plead mercy, we must plead grace, for "with you will only grace prevail." "Grace" of course refers to the unearned, unmerited, and undeserved love that God continually extends to us sinners and rebels. Many people have tried to explain God's love according to one system or another, some basing their speculations on our earning God's favor with works, or Christian character, some others trying to say that God is compelled by our inner devotion to recognize and to respond to the "innocence" in our inner being that God will consequently create in us.

But ultimately all such rationalizations fail. God is not *compelled* to do anything. *God loves because God simply loves!* God loves in spite of our sin, in spite of our rebellion, in spite of our unwillingness to love anyone beyond ourselves. What could we place before or give to God in order to earn God's attention or affection? Love? "We love God because God first loved us"! Good works? The power and means to do good works are the gifts of God. A good life? Perhaps before other people we could say we live a good life. We don't steal, we don't lie, we don't cheat on our spouse or on Uncle Sam, we don't break the civil and traffic laws, and so forth. But God looks at the heart, the human heart, the part of our person that, according to the prophet Jeremiah, "is deceitful above all things" — even to the point of imagining that our poor, feeble, self-centered love is the "reason" that God loves us. The deceitfulness and corruption of sin is so thorough, and "this damage is so unspeakable that it may not be recognized by a rational process, but only from the Word of God."[2]

Perhaps the most common sin of the deceitful human heart is ingratitude. Luther helps us with these words:

> *I hold and believe that I am a creature of God; that is, that [God] has given and constantly sustains my body, soul, and my life, my [bodily functions] great and small, all the faculties of my mind, my reason and understanding, and so forth; my food and drink, clothing, means*

> of support, [family] ... house and home, etc. ...
> Moreover, [God] gives all physical and temporal bless-
> ings — good government, peace, [and] security .... Much
> could be said if we were to describe how few people be-
> lieve this .... We all pass over it, hear it, recite it, but
> we neither see nor consider what these words enjoin on
> us.[3]
>
> This is the way the ... world acts, drowned in its own
> blindness, misusing the blessings and gifts of God solely
> for its own pride and greed, pleasure and enjoyment, and
> never once turning to God to [give thanks] or to ac-
> knowledge [God] as Lord and Creator.[4]

Luther is right. We do not perceive even a tithe of the blessings of God. How could we, then, even inadequately list God's
blessings on us, much less acknowledge them with a joyful,
grateful, and thankful heart? If we really believed the witness
of the Bible, we would not boast of being a "self-made man"
or woman, or that we had "pulled ourselves up by our boot-
straps." Even our drive for "success" is the use of God's gifts
for our own improvement. And time will not permit us to even
briefly discuss the other great and damaging sins of pride, will-
ful blindness, disobedience, and so forth. (I, personally, find
it all too painful.)

The end of the matter is this: "you [O God], we fear."
That is, when God confronts us with our sin through the Word,
we become aware of God's judgment and condemnation of
our sin. And, in Saint Paul's terms, we suddenly see that we
have no plea but "guilty" before the law of God, and there
is nothing more we can say.

III.

In the next stanza of our hymn, Luther explains the content of grace in terms of "hope" in God's Word:

And so I hope in God alone,
and not on my own virtues build.

> On God my heart will heedless lean —
> the God who's good, whose Word good willed.
>> This is my comfort and my shield;
>> my anxious heart by hope is stilled.

The line I have translated as, "the God who's good, whose Word good willed," is a little free. But I believe I have captured the essence of what Luther wanted to convey in his hymn. If we dare not set our hope on good works or the virtues of our character — least of all, a grateful heart — where do we set it? The good God revealed in the Word. For this is our lasting hope, that God is good and has willed good to us through Jesus Christ our Lord.

Writing about the first commandment, Luther wrote:

> *[A person's] whole heart and confidence [must] be placed in God alone, and in no one else .... We lay hold of [God] when our heart embraces [God] and clings to [God]. To cling to [God] with all our heart is nothing else than to entrust ourselves to [God] completely. [God] wishes to turn us away from everything else ... because [God] is the one, eternal good.*[5]

We dare to cry out to God in our deepest need, to urgently pray to God in every crisis and blessing, because God is *good*. God's goodness is shown by all the things we mentioned before, our life itself, the availability of meaningful work, the blessings of the field and the home, good government, good weather, and peace and security.

But these are — *at best* — only partial, imperfect revelations of God's goodness. I'm sure that many of you let loose a little grunt of cynicism when I mentioned "meaningful work" and "good government." And some of you may have thought of times of flood, drought, and war as well, times when so-called "acts of God" wiped out your home, property, or loved ones. For nature too "groans" as it "waits in eager longing" for the time when it "will be set free from its bondage to sin and death" (cf. Romans 8:19-20).

Where then do we see the goodness of God most clearly revealed? "The good God" in God's "good Word," in the scriptures — especially those that reveal to us the goodness of God in Jesus Christ. Here God's goodness shines in all its splendor. The gray and lifeless backdrop of our sinful, fallen, and imperfect world serves only to make all the brighter the refracted and multifaceted rainbow of God's grace. In the word of Christ's life, suffering, death, and resurrection alone we see that God is the only loving Good. We learned it in Sunday School many years ago, but it is still true today: *"Jesus loves me, this I know, for the Bible tells me so."* "All the rest is commentary."[6]

IV.

Luther finishes his marvelous hymn with this stanza:

> It's true that we are full of sin,
> yet God with grace is flowing o'er!
> God's helping hand no hindrance knows,
> though shame wells up within our core.
> Good Shepherd, gracious God, forgive
> your Israel's sins, her life restore!

Sin is a power at work in our being and in the world. And, to all appearances, it rules supreme. Yet the good Word of our good God reveals that it will not always reign over us and the world. In our hymn, Luther seems to compare sin to a deep cauldron of toxic liquid that erupts and bubbles over without any warning. The promise of God is that the well will not only be covered. It will be drained and demolished!

Perhaps Luther was thinking of Romans 5 as he penned his hymn:

> *Where sin increased, grace abounded all the more, so that, just as sin exercised dominion in death, so grace might also exercise dominion through [righteousness by faith] leading to eternal life through Jesus Christ our Lord* (Romans 5:21, GNB).

The power of sin is great — *but the power of grace is even greater.* Sin increased, *but grace abounded;* we are full of sin, *but God's grace is full to the brim and running over!* Compared to the tidal wave of grace, sin is a small ripple on the face of the cosmic waters. Sin's power is strong, but God's grace and love and Holy Spirit are even stronger!

But these things are only spiritually perceived and are hard to remember when our sense of sin overwhelms us. Luther wrote in a sermon dated December, 1528:

> *No confession of faith is more difficult to believe than, "I believe in the forgiveness of sins." The other confessions are completely external and lie outside of our experience and have no direct bearing on us .... But the forgiveness of sins makes a direct impact on me and on you. What do I get out of it if God has made heaven and earth, but I do not believe in the forgiveness of sins? Yes, and even more relevant, what do I get out of it if Christ died and the Holy Spirit has come, but I do not believe in the forgiveness of sins? ... But this confession has to make a direct impact on us in our own experience — I for myself, you for yourself, and individually for each one of us — we all must experience the forgiveness of sins.*[7]

Our Lord's Parable of the Prodigal Son remains to this day the paradigm for how God's goodness and grace lead us to the forgiveness of sins. You know the story. The son decides he doesn't want to live in the father's house anymore and, taking his share of the inheritance, hits the road. Out in the "real world" he discovers that his "freedom" is actually slavery to self. Perhaps his first and foremost enslavement was to the misconception of his father's character and motives. The Prodigal saw his father as a tyrant — someone whose only goal in life was to limit his son's "freedom" and keep the "good life" from him. In today's terms, the son saw his father as a "nerd" at best — and a child abuser at worst.

The Prodigal's attitude is the essence of sin. We too, before the Holy Spirit enlightens us, see God as a kind of cosmic "nerd" — a joy-robbing and freedom-depriving tyrant who took much more than he ever gave back. There is a real mystery in all this. Why should we despise and suspect the One who loves us best? I don't know. I can only tell you that it is real. Sin has caused us to be quite insane and blind when it comes to God. But with the help of the Holy Spirit, we can be restored to our rightful mind through the forgiveness of sins.

There was a surprise when the Prodigal returned. Although the father in Jesus' parable never *speaks* the Absolution, his every action fairly screams, *"Your sins are forgiven"!* First, he sees his son "afar off" (he's obviously been hoping for the appearance of his son's silhouette on the horizon day and night), rushes out to meet him, his heart overflowing in tears of joy and relief. Next he restores to his son all the rights and privileges of "sonship." Nothing was held back, though much had been squandered as he wandered. The father's own words sum up the whole: "This son of mine was dead but is alive again; he was lost and is found!" (Luke 15:24, NRSV). "And they began to celebrate."

1. Martin Luther, letter to Spalatin, quoted in Otto Schlisske, *Handbuch der Luther Lieder* (Vandenhoeck & Ruprecht, Göttingen, 1948), p. 25.

2. "The Formula of Concord: Original Sin," in *The Book of Concord: The Confessions of the Evangelical Lutheran Church,* translated and edited by Theodore G. Tappert (Fortress Press, Philadelphia, 1959), p. 467.

3. Martin Luther, "The Large Catechism (1529): the Creed," in *The Book of Concord: The Confessions of the Evangelical Lutheran Church,* translated and edited by Theodore G. Tappert (Fortress Press, Philadelphia, 1959), p. 412.

4. Martin Luther, "The Large Catechism: the Creed," p. 413.

5. Martin Luther, "The Large Catechism (1529): the Ten Commandments," in *The Book of Concord: The Confessions of the Evangelical Lutheran Church,* translated and edited by Theodore G. Tappert (Fortress Press, Philadelphia, 1959), p. 366.

6. Attributed to Dr. Karl Barth.

7. Martin Luther, quoted in *Handbuch der Luther Lieder,* p. 28.

5

The Liturgical Witness
Of Ephesians

"Christ Is Our Peace"

"Christ, The Victor Breached All Barriers"

1. Christ the Victor breached all barriers *Ephesians 2:14-18*
   in his fight to set us free;
   knocking down the best defenses
   of the ancient enmity:
   walls of words, and bars of bias,
   fences formed from fear's finesse.
   Ev'ry wall fell flat like Jéricho's,
   pulverized by love's largess.

2. Nailed above the head of Jesus,
   there the barrier, Law, we see,
   dying with him on the cross beam,
   with its legal enmity.
   Christ, by taking all the hatred
   all the human race could mete,
   turned our mutual hatred on us —
   made us one in love's defeat!

3. Christ the Victor took them captive,
   all our ancient enmities,
   race, religion, wealth and status —
   all fall shattered at his knees!

> Christ then led them, shamed and broken,
>   to his cross, where hatreds cease;
> reconciled to one another,
>   we are one in Christ, our peace.

Recent scholarship has discovered that Ephesians 2:14-18 was a hymn sung in the worship services in Ephesus and in Asia Minor, circa A.D. 80. Our hymn's emphasis falls on the *horizontal* beam of the cross more than the vertical dimension. That is, this hymn's focus is not on the reconciliation of people with God, but on *people with other people*. For Christ's death not only defeated the hostility between people and God, but also the hostility between the peoples themselves.

One writer describes the horizontal beam of the cross with these words:

> *The redeeming work of Christ is entirely contained in the word "peace." The whole preaching mission of Jesus is described [in Ephesians 2:17-18] . . . as a preaching of peace to all . . . near and far. The term . . . ("peace") in classical Greek is primarily negative, denoting the absence or end of war. But the biblical sense of "peace" in general is determined by the Hebrew word* shalom, *a much more positive and comprehensive word. It derives from a root which signifies totality, wholeness, harmony, integrity, well-being.* **The essence of the word signifies productive and fulfilling community with others.**[1]

The fundamental teaching of our hymn is that we are not redeemed in isolation. We are set free to become a part of a larger whole, God's new Exodus community, Christ's Body, the Church. Within this new community there is "no longer Jew or Greek, there is no longer slave or free, there is no longer male and female; for all of [us] are one in Christ" (Galatians 3:28, NRSV). And Colossians 3:11 sums it up with finality: "Christ is all and in all!" (NRSV).

These statements are extremely revolutionary, considering the times:

> *Jews and Gentiles had lived as two irreconcilable peoples; there were great religious, social and political discrepancies between them. They were two peoples in permanent and mutual contempt, in constant conflict; there was no peace between them. The time that they had lived before Christ is characterized by the absence of peace.*[3]

Yet it was God's plan, now revealed in the death, resurrection and exaltation of Jesus Christ, to unite all people into one as the Body of Christ, his Church. Somehow in the cross God was working a universal peace and reconciliation between the people of every race, people and tongue — all united to Jesus Christ through baptism and faith. On that first Good Friday, both groups, Jews and Gentiles, found an excuse to heap their hostility on the Son of God. Both groups had their representatives — Pontius Pilate on the one hand and the priestly bloc on the other — and both groups betrayed him, the one politically, the other religiously.

By taking upon himself the hostility of both groups, Christ *killed* the hostility, and made the formerly separate and estranged groups *one*. As both peoples were united in their rejection of Christ, so now they are united by him into one new, whole, reconciled, and integrated fellowship of *shalom*.

In other words, racism is dead. And so are ethnocentricity and xenophobia. These great and shameful sins are perhaps the clearest evidence we have that the universe as God planned it has suffered a complete breakdown. If peace — that is, *shalom* — is the ideal that God envisions for creation, then racism is the complete and diabolical opposite. If the world of human beings is an organism, then it is a body at war with itself and well on its way to complete disintegration. Like the victims of certain metabolic disorders, the human social order has turned in on itself, devouring itself bit by bit.

You think these metaphors too violent, too harsh? I do not think they are violent enough. Who could make metaphors violent enough for us to feel the madness of "ethnic cleansing" and tribal genocide? We do not have to go far in our own history to see the same forces at work.

The early church was aware of these realities too. As the Jewish preachers moved into the largely Gentile world of first century Rome, they encountered a mixed bag of races, languages, cultures, and religious persuasions. Although they were occasionally appalled at certain pagan practices, they did not reject this cultural richness outright.

One of Paul's sermons includes these words:

> *The God who made the world and everything in it, [the One who] is Lord of heaven and earth, does not live in shrines made by human hands, nor is [God] served by human hands, as though [God] needed anything, since [God is the One who] gives to all mortals life and breath and all things. From one ancestor [God] made all the nations to inhabit the whole earth, and . . . allotted the times of their existence and boundaries of the places where they would live, so that they would search for God and perhaps grope for [and find God]* (Acts 17:24-27, NRSV).

This and other scriptures reveal to us that cultural and linguistic variety are God's idea, born out of infinite creativity and wisdom.

How did Christ accomplish the mighty act of reconciliation and peace between the peoples of the earth? The only answer the scriptures give us is the cross. We who were raised in the church are very familiar with the Bible's teaching of how Christ "became sin on our behalf" on the cross, and by bearing its curse and rejection enabled us "to become the righteousness of God." The cross is also the place where Christ overcame death by dying.

But the cross also has a social significance. Somehow on the cross our Lord absorbed all the hostility, rejection, ridicule, suspicion, and irrational violence — *and killed them forever.* By taking upon himself the mutual hostility of the Jewish and Gentile worlds, Christ killed the hostility and made the two formerly estranged peoples *one.* Not only was our individual sin buried with Christ in Baptism; our social sins also found their Armageddon in the physical disintegration of our Lord's cross.

Put another way, as both peoples were united in their hostility toward Christ and their rejection of him, so now they are united in him into one new, whole, reconciled family and fellowship. Indeed, Paul makes the astonishing claim that once incorporated into Christ's Body, we are all members of one worldwide and timeless organism, the Church. The result is that we no longer need to remain separated and impoverished. In Christ there is no longer Jew or Gentile, Vietnamese or Black, Latino or Caucasian; we are *one new humanity* through the cross.

Does this mean that someone's cultural identity or native language needs to be discarded? God forbid! We have already established that cultural, racial, and linguistic diversity is God's idea. Nothing needs to be thrown away.

One author explains the new situation this way:

> *Through the third other [that is, Christ] the* we *and the* they *will be able to see each other in a new way — in what they really are as human beings and not as masks or categories which society has superimposed* (sic) *on them. In the new us, differences will continue ... [but] the differences will be seen in terms of inherent values in each one that can be used in the service of others — not in terms of dependence and exploitation, but in terms of inter-dependence and cooperation.*[3]

Let us pray:

> *O God, you created all people in your image. We thank you for the astonishing variety of races and cultures in the world. Enrich our lives by ever-widening circles of*

fellowship, and show us your presence in those who differ most from us, until our knowledge of your love is made perfect in our love for all your children; through your Son, Jesus Christ our Lord.[4]

1. Harold H. Ditmanson, *Grace in Experience and Theology,* (Augsburg Publishing House, Minneapolis, 1977), p. 231. Emphasis added in the last sentence of the quote.

2. Jiménez, Pablo, A., "Exégesis y exposición de Efesios 2," in *Vida y pensamiento* (Seminario bíblico latinamericano, San José, 1988), Vol. 8, Número 1, p. 18.

3. Virgillio Elizondo, *Mestizaje: The Dialectic of Cultural Birth and the Gospel* (Mexican American Cultural Center, San Antonio [TX], 1978), p. 469.

4. "The Variety of Races and Cultures," in *Lutheran Book of Worship* (Augsburg Publishing House, Minneapolis, 1978), p. 42.

7

The Liturgical Witness
Of Colossians

"The Triumph Of The Cross"

"Over The Deadline"

1. O'er the deadline once too often Colossians 2:13-15
    we with free-bound feet trespassed.
  O'er we passed from Light to Darkness
    to the realm where Death speaks last,
  easy prey for human wisdom,
    and what passes for the Way,
  till Christ trespassed our trespasses,
    blinding Darkness with his Day!

2. Nailed above the head of Jesus,
    dying with him on the tree,
  reads our record of indictments,
    ev'ry one a just decree.
  As Christ died to Law and judgment,
    so — joined with him — so did we;
  as Christ raised up serves God only,
    so we live in liberty!

3. Christ the Victor took them captive,
    all our ancient enemies,
  Sin and Law and Death and Satan,
    stripped their pow'r, their weapons seized.

Christ then led them, shamed and broken,
    in his cross's triumph-parade;
we're among the spoils he's taken,
    hope's freed pris'ners, unafraid.

This hymn is a translation and versification of the hymn Paul quotes in Colossians 2:13-15. What better way to relate to people he had never met than for Paul to base his thoughts on a lyric poem both he and the congregation at Colossae knew well. This made the sharing of his often heavy theology a little easier.

Let us begin with stanza two of our hymn. Here we are asked to envision a handwritten record — an indictment — listing our many sins. These would be read in open court as a formal charge against us. In the normal court proceedings of Paul's day the indictment would be read aloud in the presence of a judge, who, after due deliberation, would pronounce the sentence.

In our hymn we discover that God did two things to release us from the record or the indictment of our sins. First, "God crossed out" (or, better, "X-ed out") "the indictment . . . against us." When an indictment was cancelled in the ancient courts, the judge pronounced a "not guilty" verdict with these words: "Let the handwriting . . . be crossed out." At this point a large "X" would be scrawled over the list of crimes on the indictment before the eyes of all, and the case was dismissed. The record was erased, blotted out, obliterated.[1]

Now this is Good News in itself. But the next metaphor we encounter in our hymn is even more powerful. Read stanza two again. According to these words, God not only *crossed out* our sin and guilt, *he killed them.* Because the Law gives sin its power, and death its power through sin, we are often described in the letter of Paul as "dead in trespasses." So God provided a way to have the very instrument of death neutralized, taking the now "X-ed out" record of our sins *and nailing it to the cross with Christ.* Perhaps the writer of the hymn was thinking of the placard nailed above Christ's head on the cross, the list of his (supposed) crimes against the State: "This is Jesus, the King of the Jewish People" (Luke 23:28). As King of the Jewish People, Jesus rules over the Law. When Christ died, then, he died to the record of our infractions against the Law. And since we have been joined to Christ's death in our Baptism (Colossians 2:12-15), *as Christ died to the Law, so we have died to the Law with him.*

Luther expressed this same idea with these words:

> *When we were created by God the Father, and had received from [God] all kinds of good things, the devil came and led us into disobedience, sin, death, and all evil. We lay under God's wrath and displeasure, doomed to eternal damnation, as we had deserved. There was no counsel, no help, no comfort for us until this only and eternal Son of God, in his unfathomable goodness, had mercy on our misery and wretchedness and came from heaven to help us. Those tyrants and jailors now have been routed, and their place has been taken by Jesus Christ, the Lord of life and righteousness and every good and blessing. He has snatched us, poor lost creatures, from the jaws of hell, won us, made us free, and restored us to the Father's favor and grace. He has taken us as his own, under his protection, in order that he may rule over us by his righteousness, wisdom, power, life and blessedness.*[2]

This is most certainly true.

When we come to the third stanza of our hymn, we find that *all* of the Powers were attacked and overcome: Sin, Death, the Law, the devil, false religious notions, institutional power of every sort, whether political, economic or religious authority, set against Christ.[3] Yet their power is broken and their prisoners set free by the shame and defeat of the cross. Dramatic to be sure. But what irony and paradox! Honor through shame; liberation through bondage; victory through defeat; power through weakness!

The words of stanza three are full of drama and warfare, since they attempt to describe the greatest conflict of power in history: *the monumental struggle of Christ with all the Powers at the Battle of Skull Hill.* Hardly anything but a modest hillock by any standard, Skull Hill became a clashing point between God and all that opposes the Kingdom.

Our hymn goes on to depict Christ in the role of a Roman *Triumphator,* or Victor, the highest honor the Roman state could confer on anyone. The dramatic high point of the ceremony surrounding the recognition of the new *Triumphator* was his victory parade. The parade route would be lined with thousands of cheering citizens, all bursting with impatience to see their hero.

The Roman triumph unfolded before the bystanders' eyes in this order: 1) captured arms and spoils of war, pictures of battle scenes and of towns conquered, boards with names of people subjugated; 2) gifts of honor presented by conquered peoples; 3) chained prisoners; 4) magistrates and senators; 5) the *triumphator* in a chariot with his younger children; 6) Romans liberated from slavery; 7) soldiers wearing laurel-wreaths on their heads and singing ribald songs at the expense of their commander.[4] (It must have been quite a "photo opportunity.")

To the Roman mind, however, the idea of victory through death on a cross would have been perceived as the photo's negative: the dark would seem light, and the light dark. And even the church finds the whole idea difficult, even though our picture of the cross is fully developed in the rainbow colors of the resurrection.

Perhaps the irony and paradox of the cross' victory is best expressed this way:

> *As [Christ] was suspended there, bound hand and foot to the wood in apparent weakness, [the Powers] imagined they had him at their mercy, and flung themselves upon him with hostile intent. He grappled with them and mastered them, stripping them of their armor in which they trusted, and held them aloft in his outstretched hands.[5]*

The *cross*, of all things, is pictured as Christ's victory chariot from which he drives his enemies before him in the *Triumphator's* victory parade. Before Christ the enemy's best weapons, death and its fear, are displayed as the weak and defeated things they are. The place of Christ's ultimate defeat — Skull Hill — becomes the place of ultimate victory.

Thanks be to God!

1. Adolf Deissmann, *Light from the Ancient East* (Hodder & Stoughton, London, 1927), pp. 332-338.

2. Martin Luther, "The Large Catechism (1529): the Creed."

3. See Walter Wink, *Naming the Powers* (Fortress Press, 1984) for an expanded study on the meaning of the terms used for the Powers of the New Testament, especially in Colossians and in Ephesians. Based on his study and my own experience, I fully agree with him that the concept of the Powers goes far beyond "spiritual" powers to every concretion of power known to human beings: political, economic, religious, educational, social, military, and so forth.

4. Walter Wink, *Naming the Powers,* p. 56, footnote #46.

5. F. F. Bruce, *The Epistles to the Colossians, to Philemon, and to the Ephesians* (Wm. B. Eerdmans Publishing Company, Grand Rapids, 1984), pp. 110-111.

8

The Liturgical Witness
Of The Thessalonian Letters

"Come Soon, Lord Jesus!"

"As For God's Times And Seasons"

1. As for God's times and seasons   *Thessalonians 5:1-10*
       you need know nothing more,
    except our Lord's returning
       is soon — he's at the door!
    For like a thief at midnight
       who suddenly breaks in,
    Christ will — and unexpected —
       break through the night of sin.

2. The Day will soon be dawning,
       O Children of the Light!
    Let darkness' works be cast off,
       and sin's remaining blight.
    Yet we are not in darkness,
       O Children of the Day!
    Let's keep awake and watchful
       lest back to night we stray.

3. Yet we have not been chosen
       for wrath's rejecting word,
    but chosen for salvation
       through Jesus Christ, our Lord.

God's Chosen, Christ, died for us;
  we, raised with Him, life see.
So whether dead or living
  we with our Lord will be.

I.

They will start soon. All those "end of the world" prognostications. Soon there will be a blizzard of books and articles and television specials about the end of the millennium. There will be speculations about the future of technology or of space travel or of world economic trends. Some, I suppose, will be "info-mercials" encouraging you to invest your money in the "coming new age of prosperity."

But the religious speculations will be the wildest, if history is a reliable witness. For with the arrival of the twentieth century (1900) there was a huge outpouring of written material about the "signs" of the times. Every verse in Revelation, for example, was picked clean in a frenzied gleaning aimed at showing a concrete historical fulfillment of every beast, bowl, and plague.

And don't think that it can't happen again. While I was serving as pastor in South Dakota in the '80s, the aurora borealis made a rare appearance in our northern skies. The weird, green-yellow streamers were faint, but still substantial enough to obscure the stars. I saw it myself, slow-moving wreaths of ionized air. I was puzzled, but not alarmed.

The reaction of some people, however, was extreme. What seemed the most odd reaction to me was the sheer *terror* this atmospheric phenomenon evoked. Many people were convinced that this was the "sign" of Christ's return and the end of the world. In a few cases, people rushed to church to await Jesus' return "in the clouds of heaven." Dawn brought an end to the aurora borealis — and to the emotions it caused.

People, then, look for signs, especially the sign of Christ's return. Indeed, people have wanted to know the exact day and time of Christ's second coming from the very start. Even the first disciples asked: "Lord, is this the time when you will restore the kingdom?" [Jesus] replied, "It is not for you to know the times or periods that the Father has set" (Acts 1:6-7, NRSV). Our Lord's words seem to have been written with our time in mind. Go to almost any Christian bookstore and you will find dozens of books written in just the last few years that attempt to pin that exact time — or at least the season or period of time — down.

If you read too many of them you may begin to doubt the whole thing and say with the cynics, "Where is the promise of this coming? . . . All things continue as they were from the beginning of creation!" (2 Peter 3:4, NRSV). Every "prediction" has failed and Christ has not yet come. "Where is the promise of his coming! *Is the promise still reliable?"*

II.

I believe so. Paul, following Jesus, gives us much more reliable guidelines than the geysers of human opinions gushing forth today. Paul compares the Lord's return to a cat burglar's sudden and unexpected break-in.

> For like a thief at midnight
>   who suddenly breaks in,
> Christ will — and unexpected —
>   break through the night of sin.

There is nothing to indicate when or where the thief will make his move. But suddenly he is inside your house, taking your VCR, jewelry, cash, and anything else that is easily "fence-able."

Paul's teaching echoes Jesus, who said:

> As the lightning comes from the east
>   and flashes as far as the west,
>   so will be the coming of the Son of Man . . . .
> But on what day and hour
>   no one knows . . . .

Keep awake therefore,
    for you do not know
on what day, or at what hour,
    your Lord is coming.

For if the homeowner had known
    the time of the night the thief was coming,
he would have kept awake and kept watch,
    and not let his home be violated.

Therefore, be prepared,
    for you do not know
at which hour
    the Son of Man is coming. *(Matthew 24:27, 36, 42-44, CM)*

The gist of the matter is this: The second coming is real, and neither Paul nor Christ himself doubted its reality. And that it would be sudden and at a time unexpected, both underscored. However, neither speculated on the exact time of the Lord's return, *nor did they encourage us to do so.* Certain broad signs are mentioned, such as, "when the fig tree begins to blossom, expect a harvest." But anyone who farms or gardens knows there are a lot of factors that delay or hasten the time of harvest: the amount of rain and sunshine, bugs, diseases, the amount of fertilizer, hail, wind — you get the idea.

III.

The second coming, then, was never intended to be an exercise in endless — and futile — speculations on minute details from the prophetic corpus. *The New Testament's concerns with respect to our Lord's return are, in general, two: first, ethics; and, second, hope.*

1. The preferred ethical response to the teaching about Christ's return is found in the second stanza of our hymn. Here Paul uses the metaphors of day and night to give our mind's eye the overall concept.

The Day will soon be dawning,
O Children of the Light!
Let darkness' works be cast off,
and sin's remaining blight.
Yet we are not in darkness,
O Children of the Day!
Let's keep awake and watchful
lest back to night we stray.

The danger is that we might somehow drift back under the influence of Darkness and fall asleep in sin again. Yes, it is true that through Baptism and faith we have been delivered from the tyranny of Darkness and expatriated into the Kingdom of God's Beloved Son in the Light (cf. Colossians 1:12-14). But the Darkness is not passive. It remains a metaphor for the aggressive and imperialistic activity of sin, death, unlawful self-indulgence, and negligence of the Light.

And so Paul's call goes forth: "Become what you already are! You are in the Light, not in the Darkness. Other people fall asleep at night, get drunk at night, and practice secret, shameful things at night. But you belong to the Day and are meant to live in faith, love, and hope, things which only flourish in the Light of Day. *You are children of the Light, and children of the Day.* The Darkness is no longer your home nor your ultimate goal. For God did not destine us for wrath, but for salvation. Encourage each other with this thought."

2. And with this thought we have already touched on the second concern of the New Testament with respect to the Lord's return, hope. In our Entrance Hymn we have already celebrated our hope, a hope that endures in the face of the greatest losses.

1. We grieve, but not as others
who do not hold our Hope;
who unbelief has blinded —
in death's despair they grope!
For, since we trust that Jesus
was dead and then arose,

so God will bring, through Jesus,
God's dead, freed from death-throes.

3.   So comfort one another
with this, our living Hope,
and let its expectation
be seen in widest scope:
For whether dead or living,
we with our Lord will be,
from Sin and Satan's power,
from Death's despair — set free!

Christ's return is a thing of great comfort. It speaks to the deepest longings of the Christian that there will finally be an end to sin, death, the condemnation of the Law, and the power of the devil — that nothing will ever again hinder or obscure our relationship to the living God in Jesus Christ.

3. It also means that nothing will ever again separate us from kith and kin. It is not merely wishful thinking for the Christian to say, "I will see this person again at Christ's return." It is a statement of hope based on the sure and certain events of our salvation: the life, suffering, death, and resurrection of Jesus Christ. Christ's return will be the culmination, the consummation, of all of the promises.

Still, we greatly miss those who have died. And we grieve just like everyone else. Yet our grief is not the same. The non-Christian's grief is poisoned with despair. They have no hope beyond the grave, which seems to be the End. But the Christian's grief is mixed with a sure and certain hope. For we believe that the grave is a temporary resting place until Christ comes again. Those who have died (Paul says, literally, "fallen asleep") will be bodily raised, and we who are alive will be "caught up," and so we and Christ and every Christian will be with the Lord forever.

Here is the best commentary on our hope, a passage from Romans 14:

Not one of us to herself lives,
not one of us to himself dies.

If we live, to the Lord we live;
    and if we die, to the Lord we die.
Whether we live, whether we die,
    we are the Lord's, of this we're sure.
For Christ once died, but lives again,
    to be the Lord of Life and Death. *(Romans 14:7-9, CM)*

"Comfort one another with these words." For your grief is mixed with hope, a hope that will never disappoint us. Thus Paul can write:

May the God of peace ... sanctify you entirely;
    and may your spirit and soul and body
be kept sound and blameless
    at the coming of our Lord Jesus Christ.
The one who calls you is faithful,
    and he will do this.

(1 Thessalonians 5:23-24, NRSV; strophic arrangement, CM)

Amen. Come soon, Lord Jesus.

9

The Liturgical Witness
Of The Pastoral Letters

"God's Salvation Manifest"

January 26 is the day in the church year set aside to commemorate three of the early church's missionary leaders, Timothy, Titus, and Silas. If you read the book of Acts you will see their names over and over again, usually in some relationship with — and sometimes in opposition to — Paul. Three of the letters that Paul sent to Timothy and Titus still exist: 1 and 2 Timothy and Titus. All three of these letters champion the need to cling "to the standard of sound teaching that you have heard from me [that is, Paul]" (2 Timothy 1:13, NRSV). This teaching consists of "the grace given to us in Christ Jesus ... [now] revealed through the appearing of our Savior" (2 Timothy 1:9-10, NRSV).

One of the forms this "standard of sound teaching" took was the congregational hymn. In the letters of Paul to Timothy and Titus he quotes four of them. The first of them — which we sing a little later in the service as a part of the Preface to Holy Communion — is a hymn about Christ's person and work. In six curt lines, in a kind of code, this hymn worships God made flesh who died and rose again on our behalf.

In the flesh was manifested,
   in the Spirit justified.
By the angels was seen also,
   to the nations was proclaimed.

In the world was then believed on,
and in glory taken up.

But for today we will concentrate on the three *other* hymns recorded for us in the Pastoral Letters, hymns we have already sung in our liturgy as the Entrance Hymn, and Hymn of Praise, and the Hymn of the Day. These are fine examples of the so-called "Epiphany-Hymn."[1] (Please keep your copy of these hymns before you. We will be referring to them frequently.)

I.

Even a brief glance at the contents of these hymns will demonstrate how they earned the moniker "epiphany." Over and over again the synonyms for "epiphany" sprout up like tender shoots in springtime. They include the terms "manifestation," "appearing," and "revealing" — all words that imply that something that was once hidden is now seen.

And what is now revealed that once was hidden? First of all, God's fatherly, or as we might say today, God's parental and loving heart. Every one of the Epiphany-hymns is adamant in its conviction that our salvation originates in the plan and the grace and the love of God. Our salvation was no last-minute improvisation. For God gave us salvation "before all time began." We've been on God's mind forever! And at the right and proper time, "in our Time," God acted on our behalf.

The Hymn of Praise ("The Goodness And The Graciousness Of God") is especially lavish in its descriptions of God's inner motivations. The very first line states the first and foremost reason for God to act on our behalf, God's "goodness and graciousness." These words are not usually connected with God. They are, for the most part, employed when someone wants to compliment or praise another human being. Our expression, "the goodness of his or her heart," comes closest to the meaning. God acted out of the goodness of a father's heart.

In the first sentence of this hymn these terms are used to describe the ground or the foundation for our salvation:

*God is good, and has chosen to act toward us with gracious-
ness and kindness.* There is no other reason for God to be-
have toward us as God does, except that God is good. Indeed,
our three hymns make it very clear that we are saved not by
"our own weak works or efforts" or "through our good works,
but through God's grace," through a *"flood of love"* gushing from the Father's heart. We are cast helpless — but not
hopeless — upon the grace and mercy of God.

A later hymn writer put it this way:

> Nothing in my hand I bring;
>   Simply to thy cross I cling.
> Naked, come to thee for dress;
>   Helpless, look to thee for grace;
> Foul, I to the fountain fly;
>   Wash me, Saviour, or I die.   *(Augustus M. Toplady)*

II.

And naked and helpless we are. Our great enemies, sin and
death and the condemnation of the Law, have invaded God's
good creation and taken it captive. Oh yes, it is true that we
are willing slaves. For in our ignorance of God's goodness and
love we have chosen the way of death.

Yet our hymns proclaim a mighty deliverance from these
ancient enemies. One uses the familiar metaphor "justified by
grace" — leading to the hope of eternal life. Another hymn
describes us as "redeemed from sin."

But the strongest and most complete celebration of God's
victory is in our Hymn of the Day ("God It Is Who Saved
And Called Us"). Here we read:

> With th'appearing of Christ Jesus,
>   God's salvation's manifest,
> who, through Christ's death, death abolish'd,
>   blotting out death's last bequest.
> Life immortal through the Gospel! —
>   now revealed as God's great plan.

239

The last bequest — the last will and testament — of death is, well, death. This is our inheritance apart from Christ Jesus, the Lord of Life. But when God calls us to faith in Jesus Christ through the preaching of the Gospel, death's inheritance is cancelled, annulled, destroyed, overthrown, and abolished. Death's rule of tyranny has been handed down from one generation to another for millennia. But Death's kingdom was overcome on the third day when God raised Jesus from the dead and exalted him to the place of all authority and power, at God's "right hand." From there Christ will rule until even death, the last enemy, submits.

It is true that Christians still die. This is as plain as our church's next funeral. Even Paul, the one quoting all these life-filled hymns in 1 and 2 Timothy and Titus, knew that his own death was upon him.

> The time of my departure has come.
>   I have fought the good fight,
>   I have finished the race,
>   I have kept the faith.   *(2 Timothy 4:6-7, NRSV)*

Yet those who have received the assurance of "life and immortality through the Gospel" do not die in despair. For Paul goes on:

> From now on there is reserved for me
>   the crown of righteousness,
> which the Lord, the righteous judge,
>   will give me on that day,
> and not only to me but also to all
>   who have longed for his appearing.   *(2 Timothy 4:8, NRSV)*

III.

This last appearance or manifestation of Christ will not be like the first, when he came to suffer and die. The second epiphany of Christ will be in open power and glory and honor. The clearest reference to Christ's second coming is in the second stanza of the Entrance Hymn ("The Grace Of Our Great Savior, God"):

240

Our blesséd hope we now await —
th'appearance soon and glorious
of our great God and Savior, Christ,
who gave himself for all of us.

Note that this will be the same Christ who was crucified, who died, and who was buried. Then he arose from the dead. And when he arrives again, sin and death will come to an end. At that time the consummation of God's work of creation and redemption will be actualized and made concrete. It is true that the decisive battle against sin and death was fought on Skull Hill some 2,000 years ago. Yet, though defeated, our great enemies have raged on. Like desperate, cornered terrorists, they do not intend to be captured alive, but are intent on taking many others with them before they are themselves cut down.

Yet, even in the face of death, we have hope. For death will not have the final word, but will yield its power and kingdom to the One who has proven himself to be stronger than death, God revealed in Jesus Christ. Paul put it this way in another place:

We grieve, but not as others
    who do not hold our Hope;
who unbelief has blinded —
    in death's despair they grope!
For, since we trust that Jesus
    was dead, and then arose,
so God will bring, through Jesus,
    God's dead, freed from death-throes.

Our holy Hope's not anchored
    in hollow human thought,
but in the revelation
    of all that God has wrought:
Behold, then, at Christ's coming,
    we who are still alive
will not greet Jesus only,
    but those he will revive!

For Christ himself, descending,
   will cry the great command,
and at the trumpet's fanfare,
   the dead in Christ will stand!
Then those alive are caught up
   to join the living cloud,
to be with Christ forever,
   released from death's tight shroud.

So comfort one another
   with this, our living Hope,
and let its expectation
   be seen in widest scope:
For whether dead, or living,
   we with our Lord will be,
from Sin and Satan's power,
   from Death's despair — set free! *(1 Thessalonians 4:13-18;*
5:8-10, CM)

Amen. Come soon, Lord Jesus!

---

1. See Charles M. Mountain, "The New Testament Epiphany-Hymn," in *The Hymn: A Journal Of Congregational Song* (The Hymn Society in the United States and Canada, Ft. Worth, April, 1994), pp. 9-17, for more details.